Making the Most of
RHODODENDRONS AND AZALEAS

Christopher Fairweather

First edition published 1993, in the UK, by
Burall Floraprint Limited
Wisbech
Cambs
PE13 2TH

British Library Cataloguing in Publication Data
A catalogue record for this book is available from the
British Library

ISBN 0–903001–66–7

Floraprint books are published by Burall Floraprint
Limited, Wisbech, PE13 2TH

© Burall Floraprint Limited, 1993

Picture Credits
All photographs by Burall Floraprint or the author.
The author wishes to thank the following for allowing the
use of the gardens for photography: Exbury Gardens,
Glendoick Gardens, Perth and Longstock Park, Hants.

Front Cover: 'Jean Marie de Montague'
Back Cover: 'Virginia Richards'
Page 1: 'Scintillation'

Edited, typeset and indexed by Jane Robinson
Line drawings by Alan Payne

Printed in Singapore

Contents

Foreword

Anyone who has already picked up this book and opened it is hardly going to need me to tell them what wonderful plants rhododendrons and azaleas are! But there may still be pleasure in hearing me sing their praises. There may be interest too, in hearing their fascinating history.

For the benefit of those who are growing these plants, or look forward to doing so, the greater part of the contents of this book aim to help in the choice, use and care of our brilliant subjects.

You are sure to enjoy having these wonderful plants in your garden – or perhaps among your rockery, on your patio or in your conservatory. When you have chosen the suitable place, and selected the plant to go in it, you have suddenly created something very beautiful around your home.

The satisfaction will be yours probably for many years, because these are long-lasting plants. And while most other dreams of glory fade with time, your rhododendron or azalea is going to keep growing.

Christopher Fairweather's interest and enthusiasm for rhododendrons and azaleas began in the early 1950s when he spent two years at the world-famous gardens of the de Rothschild family estate at Exbury.

After a three-year contract planting tea in Kenya, he returned to Hampshire and opened his first Garden Centre in the village of Beaulieu. This was one of the first garden centres in Britain and is still operating in his name.

To any serious gardener, Exbury Gardens, near Beaulieu in Hampshire, is synonymous with the breeding and production of high quality rhododendron and azalea hybrids and it is to there that Christopher Fairweather returned in 1968 as Horticultural Manager. Through their specialisation in rhododendrons and azaleas he had the opportunity to research and travel widely in America and much of Europe.

In 1974 he began to acquire land adjacent to his home and on this started his own wholesale production nursery, specialising in shrub propagation, including, of course, rhododendrons and azaleas.

His present activities, besides travelling, include lecturing, broadcasting on radio and television and writing books.

'Persil'

Getting acquainted with rhododendrons and azaleas

Glamour is the quality that rhododendron and azalea hybrids display in full flower. They say beauty is in the eye of the beholder, meaning there are a million opinions on the subject. About glamour there can be less argument. Even for the person who resists the magic factor, it is there.

Most people who have become interested in the subject of rhododendrons and azaleas were drawn to them in the first place by the pleasurable shock of that extravagant display. When one comes upon such a plant, in a garden full of other more reticent performers, it is like seeing the star of the show making her entrance.

The effect is unforgettable.

Even if the impact becomes less, with repetition through a thousand hybrids, our attention has been seized. This complex group of plants holds so much interest that we may become deeply absorbed in growing or studying them.

Part of the special fascination which rhododendrons and azaleas uniquely possess is that, although they may be expensive and slow to propagate, they are almost absurdly easy to cultivate. They are really simple to care for – within certain limitations – and they combine this with the most splendid visual performance. And besides their magnificence in the garden, rhododendrons and azaleas retain the mystery of belonging to a special worldwide group of plants about which much is already known, but from which fresh discoveries and new forms still arise every year.

The character of rhododendrons as a botanical genus

The *Rhododendron* genus is one of those groups of plants which presents a specially wide variety of forms and sizes and habits of growth. Including evergreen and deciduous azaleas, which botanically are rhododendrons too, the whole genus comprises nearly 1000 different species that have been discovered in the wild, identified and described. Only a small proportion of those will be dealt with in this book, where we shall focus attention on those which we can grow in our gardens in temperate climates or in some cases indoors.

Besides the profusion of species that occur in nature, there has been, astonishingly, a still greater abundance of artificially produced

The Alpenrose (*R. ferrugineum*): one of only two rhododendrons native to Europe

hybrids between those source plants. A great part of the special interest of our subject concerns why and how their breeding work has been done, and what the various hybrids that resulted have to offer us today.

Taxonomy; classification and nomenclature

What human beings have done with rhododendrons – the intricacies of breeding – can only be understood by following the history of how plants were brought back from the wild. That story in turn depends on the geographical distribution of those plants and the opening up of the areas where they can be found. You can read about these topics in the next few pages of this book, but first let us look broadly at the family tree of the rhododendron group.

It may be surprising that so much new research is going on all the time about the evolutionary connections between plants. The struggle to piece together the meaning of different characteristics employs a steadily advancing technology. A picture gradually emerges, but is not yet complete, of which plant cousin is closer akin to which.

Classification of plants centres on flower characteristics more than anything else. Rhododendrons are one of those plants in which the flower is very prominently featured, so there is a lot of scope for distinctions to be drawn in this regard, and the result is an enormous number of defined species. The arrangement of these species within an accepted botanical system is accordingly very difficult and always liable to revision. Whereas most plants are grouped by placing a manageable number of *species* within the larger group or *genus*, this cannot be satisfactorily done for rhododendrons without intermediate stages. We have to see the genus as subdivided into *series* and further – in certain branches of the group – into *subseries*.

For the purposes of this book, the most significant example of this complexity are the azaleas. These constitute *only one* of the 40-odd *series* in the *genus*. Indeed, with 75 *species* grouped into 6 *subseries*, azaleas form almost the largest single *series* (The very largest series of all comprises the "Javanicum" rhododendrons from the Malaysia region which now has been redenominated as "*section Vireya*" by Dr H Sleumer, and this has 261 species).

Geographical distribution of rhododendron species

The plants we grow exist on two different planes, you might say: in the garden and in the wild. The garden is a well-tended place, weeded and fertilised, and often in a temperate zone of the world, with

An informal planting of rhododendrons and azaleas

moderate lowland climate: like your own garden, probably. (The conservatory is a yet more artificial situation, recreating a different climate).

"In the wild", on the other hand, rhododendrons and azaleas find themselves on sites widely scattered across the globe, though mostly in the northern hemisphere. Climatic conditions range from sub-arctic tundra to tropical rain forest, emphatically including those rugged mountains within South East Asia that form one of the least explored regions of the world.

Hundreds of species of *Rhododendron* are found in those parts and many more surely remain to be discovered. The reason for nature producing so many types within a small area is the diversity of its micro-climates. The still air in the bottom of the ravines is not cold but it is drenched in monsoon rain and cascading spray, while on the crags and peaks far, far above, the frosty whistling wind dries out the soil and blows much of it away. The valley floor is shaded, sometimes all day, especially where there is room for trees, whereas the upper slopes suffer scorching heat in summer, and in the winter months deep snow.

A very different environment is enjoyed by the rich and varied group of rhododendrons found in the mountains of the equatorial Indonesian Archipelago; however, only a single species makes its home in Australia.

Africa and South America yield no native members of the *Rhododendron* genus. North America accounts for up to 27 species, and the significance of some of them (especially *R. catawbiense*) is the basis which they historically provided for key steps in hybridization. The group includes 17 azaleas; whereas Europe, with the Middle East, has only one azalea amongst its mere handful of native rhododendrons. Eastern Asia has most representatives, from Sri Lanka to New Guinea, Japan and even Siberia, the greatest number, 400 species, being concentrated around the eastern end of the Himalayan chain, in south-western China, Tibet, Burma and Nepal.

Let us look at the other particular region where amazing quantities of rhododendron species proliferate, around the South China Sea. The sort of rhododendrons that grow in Sabah, (northern end of the Isle of Borneo) where extra rain is drawn down by the effect of the equatorial rainforest, are quite dissimilar to those of mountainous eastern China. At low altitudes the climate is warmer, but high or low, we are seeing the influence of the monsoon. We note that different species grow at each

The early flowering 'Bo Peep', will display its flowers when snow is on the ground

Mixed azaleas

particular altitude, and many of the highest mountains rise above 2000 metres.

Also they vary in many other ways: for instance, some epiphytic species (e.g. *R. stapfinaum*, *R. nieuwenhuisii*, grow in the peaty accumulations of decayed plant matter that become lodged in the forks of the tall rainforest trees. And others follow different seasons of the calendar, according to their higher or lower elevations. A few of them, like *R. rugosum*, can be found in flower at virtually any time of the year, at one altitude or another.

Turning to the most easterly cluster of our subjects, the evergreen azaleas, which are virtually all members of the species *R. obtusum*, we find these grouped around the Sea of Japan. The overwhelming majority of them actually had their origin in the Japanese islands, on account of which the whole grouping has come to be known as the Japanese

Azaleas. It seems that many of the natural varieties or subspecies from which they must have sprung no longer exist in the wild. This has not come about through a savage ecological attack by humans upon the plants and their natural sites. Rather, the contrary has happened. For several centuries, the plants have been eagerly sought after by gardeners and, when found, have been so energetically hybridized between all the available plant stock, that there remain no wild originals which can be regarded as uninvolved in these artificial breeding processes. Modern genetic science has recently advanced so far that we are told it may be possible in the near future to unravel the history of these unrecorded interbreedings. Maybe we shall see the recreation of the real *R. obtusum* in its natural form and variations.

The reader may have noted with surprise that the two world areas which give rise to the greatest range

of diverse rhododendron species are not the sources of most of our garden rhododendrons. Indeed, none of the azaleas come from those areas. The explanation is that the plants which succeed best in cultivation, in the more temperate and level lands of the developed world, tend, either to belong to, or to have been hybridized from, the species which are seen on milder, less humid sites, at lower altitudes.

This observation takes us back to the point made at the start of this section. Nurserymen wanting to help us make the most of rhododendrons and azaleas from all over the world in our own gardens had to choose among this range of species and breed from them to suit our needs.

Every book on rhododendrons for the last hundred years has guessed – with undiminished conviction, despite all the new plant discoveries made in the meanwhile – that there must be a great number of new species in the world still waiting to be discovered. When found, of course they will add yet more to the interest of botanical science. At the same time they will undoubtedly extend the range of fascinating plants we can grow in and around our homes.

The origin and history of rhododendrons

A genus of plants containing thousands of known types, species and hybrids, could not exist without quite a lot of history lying behind the discovery of so many wild plants and the breeding of such a lot of cultivars. Some readers will not want to be diverted by these topics from the enrichment of their own garden or conservatory. Others will feel that the breadth and depth of a subject like this wants to be considered, and that a little background knowledge enriches ones direct experience of the plants. For those, a few pages follow on geographical distribution, on discoveries and introductions, and on hybridization.

Rhododendrons and their place in the plant kingdom

Rhododendrons belong to the Heather family, the *Ericaceae*. Within that family, they evolved from the ancestors of the magnolias, by way of plants allied to camellias. Their heritage immediately places them among the great producers of showy flowers.

Their desirability as garden plants primarily depends on these spectacular blooms, so it is surprising to learn that this emphasis on profusion of flowers leads botanists to regard them as somewhat of a primitive example of a flowering plant.

The purpose of a blossom is to secure fertilization, and where this function has to be performed by any insect, its attention has first to be attracted. The perfume of the nectar, which the flower offers as a bribe for this fertilizing service, will be one attraction. But since many insects have quite good eyes and a strong sense of colour, a flower may also attract them by visual signals.

Where the flowering season is limited and the competition for insect attention is strong, a plant may go to the trouble of a lavish visual display in order to succeed. Perhaps this was more necessary when insects first evolved these ways of interacting with plants. Certainly rhododendrons have existed for a very long time, and fossils are found from fifty million years ago which correspond closely with species still existing in nature. The indications of these fossils, and the location of the most basic forms of wild rhododendrons existing today, suggest that this type of plant first arose in the Himalayan regions.

It was a type that proved very adaptable in the range of forms which the genus was to produce, as regards the sizes of the individual plants, the number of species, and the dominance which they very often achieve in the plant ecology of the location where they thrive. This adaptability explains their wide distribution around the world.

Rhododendrons and human history

Unexpectedly, in the very first recorded interaction between a

The fragrant *R. luteum* has toxic nectar

R. ferrugineum was the second species to be cultivated in Britain

rhododendron species and human race, we find the plant changing the history of mankind rather than the other way about. Like the story of "Man Bites Dog"!

About 400 BC when Xenophon was encamped with his army on the shores of the Black Sea, his soldiers in foraging for food supplies discovered a lot of delicious honey. Unfortunately the bees had made it from the nectar and pollen of what we call Azalea pontica (Latin name *Rhododendron luteum*). The fragrance of this lovely bush, which covers the hillsides in that region, is deceptive. The nectar, and so the honey, was powerfully toxic; the army, drugged into insensibility, was thrown into disarray and Xenophon's campaign collapsed.

In the Greek language the word "rhododendron", meaning "Rose tree" was first used to describe the plant

we know as *Nerium oleander*. This is a shrub far too tender to overwinter outdoors as far north as Britain, but is much used as a tub-grown conservatory decoration. The Mediterranean Oleander continued to bear the name until the 16th century, which is about the earliest date that one finds any description of a plant to which the name rhododendron now applies.

The first European member of the genus to come to light was a plant which belonged to high altitudes, for which reason it was rather late in being discovered. Until that time mountains were thought of as terrible and frightening wildernesses where nothing desirable was to be found.

But as the Alps lost their terror, their botanical life began to be studied and *R. ferrugineum* thus made its appearance in European herbal books.

It was entered at first not under tha name, but under various others, with long and confusing descriptions in Latin which did little to clarif matters for the students of those days

The lack of logical order in the collation of the observed fact remained for a long time a grea hindrance to botanical science generally. Then in 1753 a Swedish botanist called Carl Linnaeu established the categorization o plants which is still used. Within hi system, however, the placing c rhododendrons and azaleas has beer frequently and extensively changed and is indeed again under review today.

His genus of *Rhododendron* contained five species, one of which *R. chamaecistus* has been redesignated *Rhodothamnus chamaecistus*. He proposed a separate genus for azaleas with six species, of which all but one have since been included for classification among rhododendrons, while his 'Azalea procumbens' has been removed and redenominated *Loiseleuria procumbens*.

The introduction of rhododendrons and azaleas to Britain

Over 900 species are now known, but only nine were named and described by Linnaeus, and not all of those had been brought under cultivation anywhere in the world by the mid-eighteenth century.

The first to be cultivated in Britain was *R. hirsutum* grown by John Tradescant, whose father of the same name was court gardener to King Charles I. This was followed about a century later by *R. ferrugineum*, the close relative with which it shares the rather vague popular name of "Alpine Rose". The last named species has its home above the coniferous treeline of the Pyrenees and the western Alps as far as Austria; whereas *R. hirsutum* comes from similar altitudes in the eastern Alps and Transylvania, which is a limestone region. The capacity of this species to tolerate more alkalinity in the soil than almost any other rhododendron must have contributed to its success in cultivation before soil chemistry began to be understood.

The first American species were azaleas, brought to Britain as seed in 1734. According to their descriptions, these would appear to have been *R. viscosum* and *R. calendulaceum*. In 1736 came *R. maximum*, the most widespreading wild rhododendron of the eastern United States. From the region in which it flourished most luxuriantly, becoming a tree reaching to 12m (40ft), this plant is known as 'Rosebay of the Carolinas'. It is seldom cultivated, because great space is needed to accommodate such a large, coarse plant, and it offers little show of bloom to make up for this.

The next rhododendron to be introduced into cultivation, *R. ponticum*, reached England from Gibraltar by 1763. It had been identified on the Rock not many years before, after the species had already been named for the "Pontic" region of its first discovery in what is now Turkey. This plant has naturalised so well in parts of Britain as to become in places practically a weed. But it compensates for its vigorous intrusion with a very fine and generous display of flowers.

Only about a dozen species were in cultivation by the end of the 18th century, and no hybridization between them had been done. This situation was soon to change. The next thirty years brought in about twenty new species, including the very ones on which hybridization was most to depend. These included *R. caucasicum* from Central Asia in 1803, *R. catawbiense* from the Great Smoky mountains of North Carolina, 1809, and *R. arboreum* from the Indian foothills of the Himalayas in 1811. Also, the azalea *R. molle* came from China in 1823, to become the parent of the so called Mollis hybrid azaleas. The wide range of distribution of the rhododendron genus across the world says something about its adaptability. This is not the case of an easy going plant that can live anywhere. It is more a matter of genetic variability, whereby an altered plant is soon produced to occupy a different niche in the natural ecology. This is borne out by the number of distinct species that exist. The same variability has of course lent itself to extensive hybridization by man.

Hybridization begins

The confused and evergrowing list of hybrids now probably amounts to over 8,000 which could be deemed absurdly many. Considering the number of wild rhododendron species that exist – the best part of a thousand – it might be thought unnecessary to undertake great labour to generate several thousand more kinds. The purpose of hybridization therefore needs to be explained.

Only a couple of hundred species are truly cultivable just as they are found in the wild without alteration.

R. ponticum has naturalized so well in parts of Britain that in places it has practically become a weed

Of these, only a small proportion present an attractive appearance without improvement. So something had to be done if the best was to be made of the exciting possibilities of these plants.

Hybridization aims to combine the best of appearance with the best of growing characteristics. Let us take an example. The species *R. arboreum* is rather tender for the English climate. The size and colour of the flowers are captured for us by combining that stock with the hardy, but less interesting *R. maximum* in the hybrid called 'Lady Eleanor Cathcart'.

There might seem to be difficulty, in that the hardiness of the latter species depends on its later flowering. If they don't flower at the same time, how can two plants be crossed at all? In fact, there are all sorts of tricks for persuading one or other to bring on or hold back its flowering sufficiently to permit fertilization with the intended partner.

Deliberate hybridization also requires care to ensure that fertilization takes place only with the intended partner and no other. This is normally done by neatly parcelling up the flower while it is still a tightly closed bud. Then, until the seed is safely set, the bloom is unwrapped only for the moment of introducing the selected pollen.

Even without seeing this done, you can easily guess how much time and trouble must be taken to effect a predetermined crossing in such a way. After fertilization, any resulting seed has to be collected, sown and the seedlings raised. When the young plants have been brought to flowering maturity, it is time to test and record their qualities. Only then can one begin to see whether all this effort has been a worthwhile speculation.

The first historical hybridization was a rare as well as an accidental one because of the great difference

The species *R. catawbiense* was introduced in 1809 from North Carolina

between the parents. The deciduous azalea *R. nudiflorum* and the evergreen *R. ponticum* were mated to produce *R. hybridum*, which was added to the collection of the Royal Botanical Garden at Edinburgh in 1814. There are other "Azaleodendrons" which have been produced by mating different azalea and rhododendron partners, but few of them have been cultivated. It has seemed more rewarding of effort to try to intensify

the best characteristics of quite similar plants rather than confuse them with those which were too different.

At the very time when that first Azaleodendron came into being, a Surrey nurseryman named Michael Waterer was beginning deliberate hybridization between the two American species, a pink flowered form of *R. maximum* with the newly-imported *R. catawbiense*. The lilac-magenta blooms of the latter look wonderful on Roan Mountain in North Carolina where they cover thousands of acres. However, their colour does not look so good in a garden among other flowers. The aim therefore was to exchange the flower colour, but to keep the large size of both the individual blooms and the trusses, and also the habit of flowering early before putting on new growth for the season. Unfortunately, the identity of the hybrid produced in 1810 is not traceable down to the present day and may be lost entirely.

A new phenomenon

It was in 1811 that the first specimen of *R. arboreum* had arrived in Britain. It finally blossomed in 1825, and the world of gardening was astounded. The size and globular shape of the trusses, the number and size of the flowers they contained, and above all, the pure crimson colour surpassed anything seen before.

The snag was that this plant came from tropical India. Although it grew there at an altitude of between five and ten thousand feet, it was still not accustomed to frost or cold winds. It bloomed too early to be out of danger except in the milder parts of England.

Something had to be done to make this exotic colour safe from the rigours of a European winter. So in the next year, 1826, a cross was made between *R. arboreum* and an already existing hybrid of *R. catawbiense* x *R. ponticum*. The result was named 'Altaclarense', a Latin translation of 'Highclere', which was the name of the Berkshire seat of the Earl of Caernarvon, who was backing the project.

'Altaclarense', which can still be found in some gardens, was closely followed by other famous hybrids between the new Eastern importations and the range of species already cultivated in England.

Notable among these were Michael Waterer's productions, 'Nobleanum' (*caucasicum* x *arboreum*) and 'Russellianum' (*catawbiense* x *arboreum*). Recrossing of such hybrids with their parental species was also done to intensify their characteristics. This continues today, but hybrids now are no longer allowed to be given Latin names as those were, because of the possible confusions with wild species.

The hybrid fashion

These plants were very much to the taste of the 19th century garden-lovers, because there had been important changes in the trend of landscape design.

The style of the great park, as laid out in the 18th century, was intended to show off the handsome character and great extent of the estate and the good husbandry of the owner. Towards the middle of the 19th century, the power of the English landed gentry was declining and a new brand of wealthy man was

'Souvenir of W C Slocock'

coming up. He had his business of trading or banking or manufacture somewhere in the city, but his home, where he would raise his family, entertain his friends and take his ease, would be some convenient distance out of town. There he would have a fine house not far from the railway, with a large garden but no estate.

In order that such a garden should seem complete in itself and not too much overlooked by neighbours, there was need of evergreens to close the view. These would need to be dark, which was not seen as a drawback by a society so well accustomed to wearing clothes of black material, but they wanted enlivening with vivid flowers.

These people were very fashion-conscious, and a glance at the costumes of the period is enough to suggest how powerfully the massive trusses of intensely coloured frilly blossoms seen against a dark background, would appeal to their eye. The rhododendron offers perhaps the greatest expression of Victorian taste in the plant kingdom.

Now, Disraeli's British Empire has vanished into the past, but perhaps one can still look with som admiration at the enterprise and spirit of adventure with which it pursued its success. We of a century later and in all countries, can hardly be said to have lost interest in the exotic or unexpected. New discoveries and new developments still fascinate us in the plant kingdom as in everything else.

By the turn of the 20th century the whole globe seemed to European eyes like an inexhaustible source of new things to collect, including new plant material. Tropical mountain shrubs which could not survive in temperate lowlands were greedily hybridized into hardier forms, and the possession of the prizewinner from the Chelsea Flower Show and such occasions was like a badge of success and prestige. Secrecy and intrigue surrounded the experiments for their production. The atmosphere became like that of Alexandre Dumas' novel "The Black Tulip". The recipe for the parentage of each new hybrid was almost as jealously guarded as the specimen itself.

The traces of this anxiety still show in modern rhododendron lists. The early hybrids, especially those by the Waterer family, are not fully described as regards their parentage. For example, 'Doncaster', produced in 1865 is described only as "*arboreum* x". The fact about its origin is perfectly obvious. The mysteries which are being concealed are the identity of the other parent and whether R. *arboreum* was as usual the male partner.

The Waterer family

This deliberate concealment is annoying to us, especially as it generated a lot of muddled identity among the hybrids of a genus which is already confusing and prolific enough. However, the Waterers might be forgiven for their quite large part in this secrecy because so many

The large frilly blossoms reflected the flamboyance of Victorian taste

'Sappho' was introduced in 1866 by the Waterer family

members of that family also played a positive role in the improvement of stocks.

The family owned two separate nurseries, of which the original one, at Knap Hill near Woking in Surrey, was run successively by two Michael Waterers and then two Johns. At the Bagshot establishment were two Anthonys and then Gomer, who eventually returned to Knap Hill. Their successful rhododendron hybrids, which must number in scores, include 'Nobleanum' and 'Pulcherrimum' (both 1835). 'Mme Carvalho', 'Mrs R S Holford' and 'Sappho', (all 1866), 'Pink Pearl' (1897), 'Gomer Waterer' (1900), 'Alice' (1910) and 'Lady E Cathcart' (1926).

Still on the subject of the Waterers, let us look at the "Knap Hill Azaleas". At that nursery, innumerable types of large-bloomed, scented and vigorously-growing deciduous azaleas were brought into being. The work of generations went into the crossing and re-crossing of at least seven azalea species from different parts of the world. Strangely, the results of this did not publicly emerge for three quarters of a century, but were at last made known in 1925. The vegetative propagation of these highly-acclaimed plants thereafter enabled them to be put on the market by Gomer Waterer. He was a great grandson of the original Michael Waterer and, according to the historical records of the firm of Waterers now called "Notcutts", perhaps the greatest hybridist of all.

Lionel de Rothschild, another notable name in the annals of rhododendron history, owned vast oak-shaded gardens at Exbury, on the Solent side of the New Forest, where he continued the development of the Knap Hill strains with a fresh inventiveness.

As a result, the Knap Hill an Exbury Azaleas together total over hundred different registrations wit the Royal Horticultural Society. The cover, with great brilliance, the entir colour-range of which these plant seem to be capable. The developmer of these magnificent hybrids is a stor starting in the 1930's and continuin well after the second world war. A this, and more, is chronicled in book called "The Rothschil Rhododendrons" by Peter Barber an Brigadier Lucas Phillips.

Work elsewhere in the world

This historical outline has focuse on the story of rhododendrons an azaleas within Britain. The reade must be assured that this idea ha been followed for the sake o simplicity. The full story, as told i more specialist books, is longer, mor complex and a great deal mor international.

Lionel de Rothschild used his gardens at Exbury to continue the development of rhododendrons and azaleas: 'Naomi Exbury'

Hybridization continued all over the world, 'Vuyk's Scarlet' comes from Holland

Tribute must be paid especially to the early 19th century breeding work done on deciduous azaleas, producing the famous "Ghent hybrids" of the Belgian grower P Mortier; also his later-flowering "Rustica" and "Flore Pleno" hybrids.

These involved various North American species bred with Azalea Pontica (R. luteum). Meanwhile M Koster, at Boskoop in Holland, chose to breed Chinese deciduous R. molle with R. occidentale, which comes from across the Pacific in the north-western United States.

Outstanding imagination and skill on the part of generations of Japanese gardeners were involved in originating the evergreen azaleas which we know today. Motozo Sakamoto and Kojiro Akashi are the chief individual names known to us in this connection, both of modern times, and of course Toichi Domoto and E H Wilson who brought this type of plant to the West. Dutch names figure again in this field, especially Blaauw and Vuyk immortalized in the names of hybrid evergreen azaleas which are among

those listed in this book, Koster and van Nes.

American involvement in both rhododendron and azalea hybridization has been extensive and enthusiastic, especially during the last

fifty years. Indeed the distinguished names within this activity are too many to lend themselves to a brief mention. Furthermore, their work is so vigorously continuing that this has to be regarded simply as an unfinished chapter.

The search for new species

After the enthusiasm for hybridization of the already-known species, the next development of rhododendrons was a phase of botanical exploration in search of new ones. This is an even more extraordinary and exciting story, well worthy of a book to itself. It begins with the second half of the 19th century.

Around 1850, mainly from Sikkim on India's northern frontier, Sir Joseph Hooker brought back forty-five new species. These included R. campylocarpum, R. wightii and R. thomsonii. The latter species in particular, first flowering from seed in 1857, gave impetus to fresh efforts of both hybridization and exploration.

Another key plant for further development was R. fortunei, sent

The search for new species continued. R. augustinni from China and was on sale in 1893

The dwarf, pink, species R. *pemakoense* was collected by F Kingdon Ward in Tibet

back as seed in 1856 from China by Robert Fortune. Important not only for the race of hybrid offspring it produced, it had the great value of proving hardy in the north-eastern United States as well as in Britain.

Further batches of discoveries in the Far East were made by French missionaries around 1880, like R. *delavayi*, and *fargesii*, and by Edward Madden, an Irishman. These plants were not grown in Europe until much later. However, Dr Augustine Henry did get his wonderful blue R. *augustinii* introduced and granted an Award during his lifetime and R. *racemosum* was on sale in England in 1893.

The total of known species at the turn of the 20th century was around 300, of which little more than a tenth were in cultivation. The majority of the unused species that had been described (over 200 in fact) were natives of New Guinea and neighbouring islands. There was virtually no hope for the cultivation of any such equatorial kinds of plant in temperate lands like Britain, except

under wholly artificial conditions.

Plant hunters of the 20th century

Until this time there remained to be discovered the greatest rhododendron treasure house of all. Three great rivers, only fifty miles apart, thunder through chasms 1000 feet deep in the mountainous hinterland of South East Asia, just beyond the northern tip of Burma. The Yangtze Kian is on its way from Tibet to the Yellow Sea at Shanghai, the Mekong to the SouthChina Sea at Saigon and the Salween to the Andaman Sea not far from "The Old Moulmein Pagoda" of which Kipling sang. Their gorges, drenched with rain and mist as well as the spray thrown up by the torrential streams, are crowded with different species of rhododendrons from the narrow valley floor to the wind-whipped shoulders of the mountain tops.

E H Wilson set out into this region in 1899, on the first of his four expeditions to China. He was a plant

collector on behalf of the English Nurserymen James Veitch and Sons and within two years he had sent back nearly forty new species. His discoveries over a period of twenty years included many rhododendrons one might today call indispensable ranging from the large fragrant white R. *discolor*, to the small, neat R. *williamsianum* with its pink bells which has become the parent of so many modern hybrids.

Likewise George Forrest, starting in 1904, and destined to die on his seventh expedition to the interior of China in 1932, introduced a grand total of 260 previously unknown species. Reginald Farrer also died in the course of an expedition, having spent the best part of six years in China and upper Burma. Captain Kingdon Ward began collecting in 1911 in Western China, afterward veering deeper into Tibet, Assam and Burma. His finds included two of the most spectacular yellows: the beautiful R. *wardii* and the huge-leafed R. *macabeanum*; but he also discovered the dwarf pink R. *pemakoense* and the scarlet R. *elliottii*, both good garden species.

Other great names could be added to the list of the plant hunters of this region: for example Rock, Ludlow and Sherriff. Between them all they brought to light more than 600 fresh species of rhododendrons. They also gave the world a noble example by their quests; and we may hope that their wonderful accounts of the glories of these inaccessible lands may still inspire future explorers to go out and find whatever species remain undiscovered until now.

Enjoying rhododendrons and azaleas in your garden

Anyone reading this book is likely to have, among the various elements of their garden, a range of shrubs. Obviously there are many ways in which these shrubs can be chosen and used. Every gardener will make his or her own selection to suit personal preference as well as the requirements of the site. You can try to borrow some ideas from your neighbours, but your needs will possibly be very different. One garden may be exposed to the wind, another may be shaded by large trees, and yet a third overrun by dogs or wild children, yet all next door to each other.

Even the soil can vary over a yard or two, particularly if excavators have worked on it. Think about the main features of your garden: paths, hedges, clumps of flowers and shrubs, and, most of all, trees. These are what determine the way the sections of a small garden are arranged, although the house has to be at its centre.

The presence of trees is beneficial to many types of rhododendron and azalea, so we may as well begin there.

Choice of trees
The factors on which the choice of tree species depends should be:
1 the fully-grown height and spread. (Avoid very large trees, such as chestnuts, beeches or cedars, for example, which will eventually become a negative asset);
2 the requirements of the roots for water and nutrition;
3 the density of shade they will produce;
4 their decorative value in all respects, and in particular their bark, foliage, blossom and autumn colouring.

The silver birch is often chosen. Its bark is admirably set off by the leaves of rhododendrons, and its light foliage lets enough illumination through. But beware of its spreading roots!

Recommended species are the marvellous white-stemmed Himalayan Birch *Betula utilis*. *B. jacquemontii* and the River Birch *B. nigra* are also worth considering for ornamental qualities of leaf and bark. The Whitebeam and sundry other types of Sorbus such as the Mountain Ash are very good, especially *Sorbus aria* 'Lutescens', with its marvellous silver leaves, and the yellow berried *Sorbus* 'Joseph Rock' with brilliant autumn foliage. The variegated leaves of *Acer platanoides* 'Drummondii' are attractive, as are the lovely shrimp-pink shoots of *Acer negundo* 'Flamingo'. Indeed there are many other useful medium-sized trees with coloured leaves, such as *Corylus maxima* 'Purpurea', the Purple Filbert. Dark masses of foliage may be lightened with the yellow of *Robinia pseudoacacia* 'Frisia' or the graceful golden *Gleditsia* 'Sunburst'. Or, on the other hand, it can be darkened with the purple leaves of *Prunus cerasifera* 'Nigra', *Malus* 'Royalty' or *Acer platanoides* 'Crimson King'. To obtain flamboyant autumnal colours, you might choose from, among others, *Prunus sargentii*, *Liquidambar styracifolia*, *Acer palmatum* 'Chitoseyama' or again *Enkianthus campanulatus*, *Nyssa sylvatica* (scarlet in autumn), *Cercidiphyllum japonicum* and the lovely *Amelanchier canadensis*. Its large-flowered hybrid cousin 'Ballerina' is a fine alternative. *Prunus tibetica* from the Himalayas looks well among rhododendrons in winter because of its shiny mahogany bark, and so does *Prunus autumnalis* with its autumn and winter flowers.

Rhododendrons and azaleas within your main shrub planting
Let us now move onto your main bed of rhododendrons. It will be more interesting to have a number of different varieties to give a range of colours in the spring. Also they might be grouped with completely different

Mixed azaleas flowering under the rich foliage of *Acer palmatum* 'Atropurpureum'

plants which flower at other times or which provide contrasting foliage through the non flowering season as described below. Finally, careful thought must be given to the dimensions of all these shrubs, and their habit of growth, whether erect or spreading or creeping, to enable them to be planted in such a way as to set off the overall mass.

When planting rhododendrons, you must of course allow each one enough room for its future growth which, as we have already seen, may reach a width of 2–3m (6.5–10ft) or

sometimes more in the case of a fairly large one.

This poses a problem, because when you buy them they rarely measure more than 60cm (2ft) high by 50cm (1.5ft) wide. Shrubs of this size would look a little silly if planted with the generous 4–6m (13–20ft) spacing they will later require. There are several solutions:

Firstly, design your shrubbery as it will be when the plants are fully grown; plant the rhododendrons in their allotted positions and fill the empty spaces between them with extra

shrubs which you would remove after a few years for repositioning. This solution implies that you have planned where to reposition the surplus at the appropriate time.

Secondly, follow the first solution but fill the gaps with plants destined to be scrapped in due course. There are many fairly cheap shrubs, which grow fast but acquire, as time goes on, a less tidy and attractive appearance. Shrubs suitable for this type of temporary association include Buddleia, Escallonia, Deutzia Forsythia, Cytisus, Ribes, Kerria Cornus and Philadelphus.

In either solution make sure that the shrubs planted in the spaces cannot in any way hinder the growth of your rhododendrons.

Finally, grow a carpet of ground cover plants between your young rhododendrons. Be careful with combinations of colours when several different shrubs are to flower at the same time. Do not use excessively bright colours but blend them with gentler shades and with white. 'Bow Bells', 'Percy Wiseman', 'Golden Torch' or 'Surrey Heath' would make an harmonious group of creams, pinks and whites.

Take care not to mix reds which clash – and this can happen, in spite of some people's idea that organic colours are automatically harmonious by some law of nature. An example of clashing like this would be between *R. impeditum* and 'Scarlet Wonder'. Problems can also occur with various badly-matched shades of pink, when some tend towards blue and others towards salmon. An example in this case would be 'Fabia' with 'Fastuosum Flore Pleno'.

The importance of foliage qualities

While nothing can be more glorious than a fine show of rhododendron and azalea blooms, it is worth emphasizing often that when their

Rhododendrons with variegation

ponticum 'Variegatum'
'Goldflimmer'
'President Roosevelt'

Rhododendrons with colourful new shoots

'Bow Bells'
'Elizabeth Lockhart'
'Pink Drift'
'Humming Bird'
'Moser's Maroon'
pseudochrysanthum
williamsianum and some direct and indirect hybrids
orbiculare
yakushimanum and hybrids
impeditum

time has passed, that particular splendour is gone. However, we need not be punished for our indulgence in that spectacle by enduring dullness in the garden for the rest of the year. We can make sure of further interest by giving careful attention to other qualities which are not restricted to the flowering season. With our subjects, that means foliage qualities.

Never forget about deciduous azaleas, and the excitement that many varieties can offer in their autumn leaf colour. Evergreen azaleas are not going to compete on quite the same level, though some do make a small contribution by turning a few of their leaves to a vivid colour among the minority of dark green ones.

Another chance of extra colour comes with certain rhododendrons which present variegated foliage. There are not many examples to consider, but they do offer quite a large bonus, to be able to enjoy that type of flower without darkening your garden so much to get them.

More subtle effects of foliage interest depend on interplay of effects between distinctively different leaves. In size there is the range from the huge *macabeanum* to the tiny *parvifolium* leaf, in shape from the long, narrow *linearifolium* to the round *orbiculare*, and we have the smooth *ponticum* and woolly *floccigerum* species. Some of these are more adaptable to our gardens than others, and some of the above species are not described further in this book, but I only want to suggest the sort of interest which this factor can add to your shrubbery.

Finally, but perhaps most interestingly, let me draw your attention to the delightful effects of young growth in rhododendrons. This often continues, well after the spring flowering is over, to show colours and textures in the young shoots quite different from the old leaves, so that two quite contrasting effects are intermingled on the same plant.

Effective plant associations – Shrubs

If you wish to have flowers early in the season, why not plant some *Daphne mezereum* in the foreground? It is very hardy and will be covered with pink flowers (white on the 'Alba' variety) which perfume the air delicately in March or even as early as February. Its attractive long, bluish leaves appear after the flowers, and its red fruits provide a new attraction in the autumn. This shrub will not grow much above 1m (3ft).

Daphne odora, or its variegated form, is worth growing for its red-tinged white flowers, which can appear in the winter if the weather is not too severe. It will perfume your entire garden at a time when you do not expect to come across spring fragrances. This plant grows best in a mild climate: elsewhere it will need a great deal of protection.

Another new Daphne, which has recently appeared on the scene from the Himalayas is the sweet-scented winter-flowering *Daphne bholua*. Two of its cultivars, 'Jane Postill' and 'Darjeeling', are both evergreen but 'Gurkha' is deciduous. All of them flower in January or February on a sheltered site.

Hamamelis mollis, like its lovely pale-yellow form 'Pallida', is a shrub of remarkable beauty and interest, which will brighten your garden in midwinter and appreciates being grown in similar conditions to the rhododendron. Its beautiful, round, deciduous leaves remind one of those of the hazel and take on splendid autumn hues; but it is in winter that the yellow and delicately-scented flowers appear on the bare wood. This erect shrub can reach a height of 4m (13ft) in time, and will form a large, light "fan" shape above the

The variegated foliage of *R. ponticum* 'Variegatum'

The dark background of evergreen trees provides a good contrast with the bright flowers of hybrid rhododendrons

squat, rounded outlines of your medium-sized rhododendrons. The coppery 'Orange Beauty' and bright red 'Diane' are two other Hamamelis to consider.

If you have space, try *Magnolia wilsonii*, a delightful large shrub which carries small, hanging, bell-shaped flowers in June. Little M. *stellata* manages to be more conspicuous and more compact. Yet another white one, with large freely borne flowers, is the vigorous 'Merril'. The latter is a *loebneri* cross, and so is the subtly lilac-pink coloured 'Leonard Messel'. One more Magnolia hybrid that wants mentioning is the ever popular 'Soulangeana' with pink and white flowers borne on the quite young plant.

Of course, the camellias should not be forgotten. They bloom well before rhododendrons and azaleas and enjoy similar growing conditions.

Their leaf-colour is not unlike that of the rhododendron, so they may mass together rather darkly in summer if care is not taken to add some other ingredient.

The heath *Erica carnea* forms a delightful green carpet all year round, and is covered with white or pink flowers in winter. Most heathers are low growing, but *Erica arborea* 'Alpina' and *Erica lusitanica* are tree heaths over 2m (6.5ft) tall. These two need a lot of shelter but are covered with delicate white blooms in winter. Their effect will be greatest at the rear of your shrubbery, under cover of a taller tree which will protect them from frost.

Taking over in July and August, pleasure is derived from the white flowers of *Stewartia pseudocamellia*, whose foliage also takes on an attractive hue in the autumn. Allow for a fully grown height of about 3m.

Low shrubs are very useful near the house or in the front of shrubberies. We have already made mention of daphnes and heathers which are so useful in this respect. Dwarf rhododendrons and low-growing evergreen azaleas can be placed among them.

The Viburnums – one species of which, the famous "Snowball Tree" (*V. opulus* 'Sterile') is known to everyone – also include a number of very interesting small shrubs such as *Viburnum davidii*, which grows no taller than 1m (3ft). It is of a rounded shape and covered with splendid, very dark evergreen leaves endowed with veins which give them relief. It is fairly hardy in Britain and has small pinkish-white flowers in June and handsome dark-blue fruits (drupes) in autumn. *V. burkwoodii* could be similarly described but is larger, flowers earlier than most rhododendrons, and lacks the fruits.

Viburnum carlesii is of a similar size. Its main interest lies in its round clusters of marvellously fragrant flowers in April and May. Their pinkish-white colour would serve to soften the brilliance of a red or bright-pink rhododendron blooming at the same time.

Viburnum 'Summer Snowflake' is an unusually long-flowering hybrid from Canada, and the larger June-flowering shrub *V. plicatum* is worthy of note for the unusual later habit of growth shown by its varieties 'Mariesii' and 'Shasta'.

One of the best small shrubs is *Skimmia japonica*, which forms a well-defined, rounded dome not more than 1.5m (5ft) approximately in height. Its male plants bloom as early as February. Later, on the female shrubs alone, there is a magnificent show of red berries, which birds do not like and therefore remain on the bush throughout the winter. One male shrub is required among every four or five female plants if berries are desired, except with the subspecies *Skimmia reevesiana*, which has a hermaphrodite character (male and female flowers on the same plant).

If you plant Junipers of any sort, it is advisable to distribute several around the shrubbery in order to repeat the characteristic effect of their foliage at various points. There are many useful species to choose from, especially low-growing or creeping ones. The *Juniper squamata* varieties 'Blue Carpet' and 'Blue Star' are particularly good.

Perennials and bulbs

Perennials can be very satisfactorily associated with rhododendrons and azaleas, but it is preferable either to choose species which form a carpet or ones with a tidy outline to avoid creating a "jumble" in the shrubbery. They must also be chosen to share the soil conditions and aspect required by rhododendrons. With these ideas in mind, and in order to obtain a decorative effect in the various seasons, one may mention a few in particular.

Hostas are plants which disappear in winter, but they reappear above ground each spring and last all summer until the frosts. Their handsome leaves form big rounded tufts with bluish, yellow or green shades. In some forms, these colours

'Hinomayo' underplanted with *Hosta fortunei* 'Albopicta'

are variegated with gold or white, which has the effect of brightening the dark masses of evergreen rhododendron foliage.

Euphorbias, hellebores and many ferns are very suitable. So are primulas, especially *Primula denticulata* and the Japanese types. Another good choice is the Himalayan Poppy, *Meconopsis*, in shades of blue, yellow or red.

Bulbs are particularly well-suited to an association with rhododendrons.

**Bulbs suited to planting
with rhododendrons and
azaleas**
Allium
Anemone
Crocus
Cyclamen
Chionodoxa
Erythronium
Iris reticulata
Leucojum
Lilium
Montbretia
Muscari
Scilla
Trillium (easily confused with
Trollius, which would also be
suitable, but is not a bulb).

Pieris, rhododendrons and azaleas all belong to the Ericaceous family

The mulch which the shrubs need provides an excellent growing medium for them.

Ground cover

Many ground cover plants can provide a luxurious carpet all through your shrubbery or simply between the rhododendrons while you are waiting for them to grow. Most of the suitable plant material would be classified as dwarf or creeping shrubs.

Everyone knows the beautiful effect of the Ivy, which is so useful in the shade. It comes in numerous varieties, some of which have light coloured or variegated leaves. Much pleasure will be given by the charming white flowers of the Creeping Dogwood (*Cornus canadensis*), and the pink blooms of *Geranium macrorrhizum* 'Ingwersen' above its appealing five lobed leaves; also by the handsome regular foliage of *Pachysandra terminalis*, the delicacy of *Tiarella*, whose dainty stalks of white flowers stand up in the spring above enchanting foliage, and finally by the blue flowers of the various forms of Periwinkle. It should be remembered too that the heath *Erica carnea* forms a neat carpet, and it flowers in the winter.

These ground-cover plants have the big advantage of hiding the soil, which would otherwise remain bare between the shrub stems. They also stifle weeds, provided that the soil was not already infested with them at the time of planting.

Rhododendrons and azaleas in all situations

I would like to encourage wider use of the versatile rhododendron family. If we consider them solely for planting in woodland gardens, then we miss many exciting opportunities. Here are a number of ideas that will give you new opportunities to enjoy these plants plus adding to the flowering season.

The Rock Garden

Some of my happiest holidays have been spent on rocky hillsides, enjoying the wild Alpine flowers that grow there so abundantly. Rock gardens seek to imitate and embroider upon the "natural gardens" found in such mountainous regions. They consist of low plants, conifers, mosses etc, growing among outcrops of stone. Without embarking too far upon this vast subject, let us note that rhododendrons are mostly mountain plants and that the dwarf species are very well suited to the rockery.

A rock garden should be sited where it will not be short of light. It may face north, but only if it is not shaded. It must be both well watered and extremely well drained.

Proximity to large trees is not very favourable since rockery plants do not like being covered with dead leaves in the autumn nor the dripping of water from branches after rain.

It is not necessary, and can even be undesirable, to use large quantities of stone. The "rocky" feeling can be created with a few judiciously placed thick slabs or boulders which will give a more natural effect than any amount of smallish stones piled up in a heap. If one is fortunate enough to have a bank or piece of sloping land it will be easy to arrange rocks on it as a sculptural relief, but a very attractive effect is possible on flat

ground. The "relief" may then be achieved by careful deployment of the plants according to their height.

Of course, the plants on the outside should not be too tall but the lowest ones – mosses and ground cover plants – need to be towards the centre. This sounds as if it might be the wrong way round but it adds to the effect of the rising rocky centre and makes it seem more natural. Some well planned gardens create

Rhododendrons with alpines

the illusion of a small valley where one can imagine seeing a stream flowing, although the ground may be practically flat. For that matter, if trouble and expense are of no concern, you could actually have a stream, with a pump to circulate the water from the bottom back to the top.

Depending on the overall scale, one may choose small shrubs such as *Rhododendron impeditum*, *R. campylogynum*, or the hybrids 'Sapphire', 'Carmen', 'Egret', or 'Pink Drift'. Several more examples are given in the Dwarf and Alpine section of the Plant Index on page 83. These can be combined with Alpine plants which I am not attempting to list here as the range of possibilities is so great. You will find it very pleasant and interesting to choose them for yourself by eye, from the Alpines table at a good Garden Centre.

In a larger-scale rockery, rhododendrons of approximately 1m (3ft)

in height and Kurume Azaleas can be beautifully combined with heathers and small conifers.

The town garden

The main function of a garden in town is to be looked at from the house, providing a haven of freshness for the eye. Sometimes it can be difficult to design if it has an uninspiring narrow rectangular shape. Or it may be cut off from the neighbours or the street by high walls which cast a lot of shade. When empty, such a garden might resemble a shoe box without a lid. In summer it may seem that all that is required to remedy this are a few trees of sufficient size, and some well placed shrubs. But for more than half of the year the effect would be very dull without evergreens.

Rhododendrons are suitable for this purpose, since they mostly tolerate conditions of life in town. When choosing varieties, look for

hardy hybrids of a medium size. In restricted space of this nature, the scale of the shrubs is a more important factor than the colour of the flowers.

Another typical characteristic of the town garden is the poor quality of the soil. Its fertility is never renewed by nature, as it would be in the country. Furthermore, it is polluted by toxic fumes and particles of chemical products suspended in the air. These fall out gradually if they are not brought down by the rain. The "soil" may even be nothing more than the garbage of urban life, including bits of cement, broken glass and scrap iron. If you are lucky, there may be a little earth in with all that, but don't be surprised if it is only clay dug out of the foundations, mixed with rubble.

If the "soil" is in this condition, the ideal solution is to replace it completely. This is expensive, so one may have to make do by adding large quantities of peat to improve its

Azalea japonicum in a town garden

Recommended list of dwarf and alpine rhododendrons

approximately 1m–1.5m (3–5ft)

'Arctic Tern'
'Bambi'
calostrotum
campylogynum
'Carmen'
'Cilpinense'
'Dora Amateis'
'Egret'
ferrugineum
'Ginny Gee'
keiskei 'Yaku Fairy'
'Lori Eichelser'
'Patty Bee'
pemakoense
'Ptarmigan'
russatum
'Scarlet Wonder'
williamsianum
yakushimanum

Rhododendrons for a town garden

'Anna Baldsiefen'
'Bambi'
'Blue Tit'
'Bow Bells'
'Carmen'
'Curlew'
'Cilpinense'
'Doc'
'Dora Amateis'
'Egret'
'Elizabeth'
'Ginny Gee'
'Golden Torch'
impeditum
'Odee Wright'
'Patty Bee'
'Ptarmigan'
'Scarlet Wonder'
'Snow Lady'
'Titian Beauty'

Deciduous azaleas for a town garden

Azalea pontica	yellow
'Ballerina'	white
'Berryrose'	pink
'Cecile'	deep pink
'Daviesii'	cream
'Gibraltar'	orange
'Royal Lodge'	red
'Strawberry Ice'	pink

Scented but tender rhododendrons for a sheltered town site

'Fragrantissimum'
'Lady Alice Fitzwilliam'

---

texture for shrub planting.

The third problem in a town garden is that of shadows cast by surrounding buildings and perhaps also by established trees. They reduce the light, thereby considerably shortening the list of plants which may be grown. Happily,because most rhododendrons prefer a sheltered position and a certain amount of shade, they generally give satisfaction in towns.

When selecting your plants, remember that the darker and shinier their leaves, the better they will resist air pollution. Also the dripping of water after rain may be detrimental to some plants. This is why azaleas are less happy in an urban situation.

The rather sheltered microclimate of the town garden often, but not always, permits the cultivation of less-hardy varieties. So readers who wish to risk growing the more delicate rhododendrons have their chance here. You would be risking the danger of a very severe winter or a late frost; but there may be many mild seasons in succession, when your plants could be giving you satisfaction, before another arctic episode occurs.

I suppose I am thinking of the unreliable mildness of England in these remarks. Readers in other countries must make allowances for what they know of their own climate.

In the town garden there are innumerable possibilities for covering the ground between your shrubs with low plants. Bergenias and hostas are among the most useful ones, and even more reliable success can be achieved with some of the true geraniums, (but don't confuse these with the 'Balcony Geranium', which is in reality a Pelargonium). A perennial which, once established, will thrive and expand without any effort on your part is *Alchemilla mollis*. The same applies to ferns, whose charm remains unequalled. All these plants prefer at least partial shade.

"Empty" periods can be filled by means of bulbs and annual bedding plants.

To finish with the subject of the town garden, it is worth noting that its use may be extended after sunset by means of artificial lighting. In addition to the fascinating general effect of flood-lighting on foliage, spotlights will emphasize the beauty of plants whose pale blooms are particularly attractive at night. This of course is an option in country gardens also but the idea probably has particular appeal for the town dweller who is fond of entertaining in the evenings.

Around the house, on the patio and in containers

Rhododendrons and azaleas for use in small beds around the patio, or placed on a terrace in pots and tubs, want to be selected for rather formal, what one might call 'architectural' qualities. Habit of growth is far more important than flowers here. It is no virtue at all for plants used in this way to be vigorous growers, but reliability is very valuable, particularly when plants may be presented in pairs which are intended to comprise a-symmetrical

Rhododendrons around the fish pond

arrangements, such as in urns or beds either side of a doorway or a flight of steps.

A few suitable plants for this type of use would include low-growing dwarf rhododendrons such as the yellow 'Patty Bee' or bright-red 'Scarlet Wonder', the white and spreading 'Ptarmigan', or the blue low-growing species *impeditum*. Evergreen azaleas are also excellent, especially the low, compact types like 'Hino Crimson', white 'Panda' or bright orange 'Squirrel'.

With their compact, fibrous rootball, rhododendrons and azaleas of dwarf and medium-growing varieties will grow happily for many years in a pot or wooden tub. Indeed, for all who garden on alkaline soil, (containing lime), this can be the easiest way to cultivate and enjoy these lovely plants. Likewise for those with colder gardens, container-growing offers the opportunity to move your plants away to a sheltered or protected site to avoid winter damage.

Your first task is to choose a suitable pot or container. A wooden tub, or an urn, or pot made of plastic or terracotta, can all be used, provided there are plenty of drainage holes in the base. This is really the first essential, and a few broken terracotta crocks or fairly large stones can be placed in the bottom, further to improve the drainage. Next, you must prepare or buy some suitable ericaceous compost. Mixing up your own recipe gives you the opportunity to provide the very best. My recommendation would be, 50% sterilised loam, 50% moss peat, plus a quantity of sharp grit or sand. Make sure the loam you use is an acid one suitable for rhododendrons.

Fill your container with compost to about two thirds of the way up and place your chosen plant into it. Then making sure that the top of the rootball finishes level with the top of the compost, fill around the root with the remaining material. Ideally the final level of the soil should be just below the top of the container to allow room for watering. The compost will sink a little after planting, but that is useful because the space can be made up with a mulch of ground bark.

By far the most important task with any container is to keep the soil moist at all times. Please remember that all rhododendrons and azaleas will suffer if the soil becomes too dry. A light dressing of balanced fertilizer, such as the long-term one with the brand name of Osmocote, will help to keep the plants in good condition. But nothing matters more than plenty of water. If you are particularly proud

Azalea 'Lullaby' on the patio

The scented, but tender, 'Lady Alice Fitzwilliam'

house, which they perfume with their delicate fragrance. The species *R. moupinense* and the hybrid 'Cilpinense' are examples of the type of small rhododendrons whose magnificent early blooms can be saved from spring frosts so that we can still enjoy the pleasure of them today as interior decoration.

Exotics – Vireyas

Of the world total of approximately 900 different wild rhododendron species about one third can be found in the Malay Peninsula and the South East Asian Islands, including New Guinea. This whole group of rhododendrons are collectively known as "Vireyas". For many years, these lovely plants have been in cultivation in the milder climates of the world – especially parts of New Zealand, Australia and the West Coast of America.

Apart from the many natural species of Vireya, superb new hybrids have been raised with very beautiful flowers, ranging in colour from white to soft pinks, and yellows to deep vibrant orange. The foliage is

of your plants and can afford it, you may wish to provide them with one of the automatic watering facilities available, and eliminate the risk of losing them by accidental neglect. Systems of this sort can be obtained from the more sophisticated garden centre.

The cold greenhouse or conservatory

Glass structures, by protecting plants from frost, give us the opportunity to

grow quite tender shrubs to perfection and to bring certain hardy ones into flower much earlier than out of doors.

The most delicate varieties of rhododendrons are particularly well suited to a cold greenhouse. Many have strongly-scented white flowers, or white with splashes of pink. Forty or fifty years ago, these plants used to be grown in pots to be taken into the

Rhododendrons for the conservatory
'Bric a Brac'
'Candy'
'Cilpinense'
dalhousiae
'Egret'
'First Light'
'Flamenco Dancer'
'Fragrantissimum'
'Java Light'
'Lady Alice Fitzwilliam'
maddenii
moupinense
'Sesterianum'
'Simbu Sunset'

'Thai Gold', one of the new, exciting, Vireya hybrids suitable for indoor decoration

Containerised growing is a good way of solving the lime problem: 'Alexander'

generally recognisable as of rhodo-dendron type, but the flowers are unusually intense in colour, and in many cases look like waxy bells in form and texture. Apart from the flowers being in some cases quite extraordinarily beautiful it is not unusual in this range of plants to bloom once in the late spring and again in the autumn.

This whole family will not tolerate frost but they will survive temperatures just above freezing and, therefore, lend themselves well to growing in a cool greenhouse or conservatory. They are happy being pot grown in an acid, open compost with good drainage. Watering should be on a regular basis but not overdone. Allow the plants to be fairly dry through the winter. Generally Vireyas prefer to be rather pot bound – so do not repot them over frequently. Some of the species and certain hybrids tend to have a rather straggly habit of growth, but they respond well to pruning.

Given frost-free conditions and a little care and attention, we have in these Vireyas a whole new exciting range of rhododendrons for indoor decoration, and many of them scented. One final bonus is, that they are generally very easy to root from cuttings.

Indoor Azaleas

Turning to azaleas, the ones with large blooms which we buy for our aunt at Christmas belong to the species *Rhododendron indicum*. They cannot withstand the British winter climate and need protected conditions.

Warmth is required to persuade them to flower in winter, but when the summer comes they can be planted out in the garden. If you do not let them go short of water, you will be able to keep them going for many years, wintering indoors. The whole range of tender Indica azaleas which are sold as pot plants could be included in the lists of Conservatory Rhododendrons, but this would not provide any information of use to the general public. When these plants are sold, they are never identified by their hybrid names, only by their obvious colour.

Unfortunately, many Indicas do not live very long. If what you are keen to do is force azaleas into bloom you may have more success with certain of the regular dwarf evergreen types such as 'Blaauw's Pink' 'Hinomayo', 'Hino Crimson' and 'Mother's Day' or 'Rex'. They lend themselves to growing under glass and provide magnificent interior decorations. These varieties have the further advantage of being hardy outdoors all the year, except in a very rigorous climate. Your cold green-house should need no added heating except in the depths of winter, and on those occasional cold spring days which are particularly harmful to the flowers.

Making the important choice

The question most often asked is, if I buy this plant, how tall will it grow? Let us concentrate particularly on rhododendrons for the garden shrubbery. There is not too much problem of azaleas becoming overgrown as they seldom rise above 1.2 or 1.5m (4 or 5ft) tall. Deciduous azaleas get somewhat taller on good soil, and could form a thicket of 3m (10ft) if pruning is neglected, but there is no need to let that happen.

With rhododendrons, potential plant-size is the key to their successful use, especially in small gardens. The setting of planting distances which allow correctly for development avoids the wasteful expense of buying plants which later become overcrowded. To choose wisely among the range, which extends from miniature species to massive, spreading trees, requires some care. The information given later in this book, about the eventual size which is normally attained by the different varieties, is intended to help you with making successful choices. These ultimate heights are given for each of the varieties individually described on page 55.

Favourable conditions of growth

For your particular specimen to fulfil expectations of the size and rate of growth usual for its variety, of course it needs to be given favourable conditions. In this connection, let us remember that certain rhododendrons are woodland dwellers and prefer to be planted in light shade. Others, specially some dwarf varieties, have arrived here from the high Himalayas, China and Tibet. There they grow on windswept hills and, therefore, feel more at home in our garden if planted in an open site.

Then, given a soil rich in humus that does not dry out, we can expect surprisingly rapid growth in a range of shrubs that are usually considered slow. It is not unusual for a rhododendron of the larger type to grow up to 45cm (18in) in one season, given optimum conditions. However, if the soil is poor and dry, and the site is exposed, then growth could be reduced to barely 4 or 5cm (2in) each year.

The plants we grow in our garden have arrived from all over the world, often originating in very much warmer climates. Accordingly, many of the more exotic types can be grown outdoors only in the milder parts of the world. Southern areas of England are well favoured in this respect, and there are also some suitable western localities in Scotland and Ireland, Warm, western coastal regions of the United States and Canada, as well as the south eastern States have also large areas where outdoor rhodo-

Here 'Blue Danube' flourishes against the wall of this house

dendrons and azaleas will thrive. Likewise in Japan and some regions of New Zealand and Australia.

Where the weather is colder, as on the continent of Europe, it is possible to give extra protection by planting under light shade or having substantial windbreaks around your garden. Indoors or in a conservatory situation, of course, plants can be grown in countries where they would never survive the rigours of the climate outdoors.

Patience will be rewarded

Please don't forget, as many do when they choose a young plant, that you should not demand the luxury of too many flowers in the first season. A profusion of blooms on a young rhododendron will restrict its growth. It is far better to have a healthy shrub in future than too many flower buds now. Allow it to get well established, and then enjoy the flowers.

Can one avoid the delay by buying a rhododendron that is already old enough to be blooming? This also has its drawbacks. A more mature specimen will often not grow away after transplanting as well as a young, vigorous one. There is no substitute for patience in gardening.

Value for money

Many of the plants described in this book are fairly slow to produce, taking three to four years in the nursery to reach a good saleable size. Propagation can be difficult too, so rhododendrons and azaleas will be among the more expensive plants you buy for your garden. Therefore, it is important that you make absolutely sure that you buy only the very best specimens, correctly identified by name and free of any disease. These plants ought to give you many years of pleasure, so it is unwise to buy cheap or inferior plants. So often, what looks like a bargain can prove to be a poor

investment, giving uncertain flowering and little growth. It's a pity to have the best spaces in your garden occupied for years by unworthy specimens.

Where to buy

In most countries where rhododendrons and azaleas can be grown, there are numerous excellent specialist retail nurseries who would supply your order. (Separate list of retail nurseries on page 107). Or perhaps your most convenient way to purchase is to visit your local garden centre and choose the very plant you want.

Again, I would like to repeat the

warning, not necessarily to choose plant covered with buds. Of cours you want to see the flowers as soor as possible, but it is asking too muc of our young plants to expect a mas of flowers and vigorous growth at th same time. Allow the plant to grov first, and the flowers will follow late

When to buy

The optimum time to buy and plan is from early autumn through t spring. Since virtually all plants no sold at garden centres are offered i pots or containers, it is possible t obtain them during all months of th year, but you should avoid plantin

A profusion of flowers on a young plant will restrict growth. 'Fantastica' is well established here so we can enjoy the flowers to the full

hen the ground is very dry or during
spell of frost. If you find you have
ought or been given a plant when
eather conditions are not good for
lanting, keep it under cover where,
watered, it can stay for many weeks
ntil things improve.

Hardiness ratings

ou will naturally want to choose
lants that will be hardy in your
articular site. So far as possible, I
ave indicated, for each plant named
n this book, the Hardiness Rating as
sed by the Royal Horticultural
ociety. There are similar ratings as
sed by the United States Depart-
nent of Agriculture. Unfortunately,
ue to changes that have begun but
ot yet applied overall, these
American ratings are not available
n every case. Those known are shown
n the descriptive lists, with the British
ating H1–5 in <u>increasing</u> order of
ardiness to the right of the flowering
nonth, and the American rating in
<u>decreasing</u> order of hardiness to the
ar right. An explanation of these
atings in general terms is given
elow, but they need to be interpreted
or your practical use with a certain

'President Roosevelt' is valuable for its variegated foliage as well as its flowers

amount of common sense: as whether
your garden is a high altitude, for
instance, or in a frost pocket or
exposed to much wind.

Leaf qualities

The subject of leaf qualities, and the
important contribution they can make
to the all-year-round interest of the
garden, has been discussed above in
general terms (page 22). There is a
tremendous variation to be seen in
the size, shape and colour of different
rhododendrons.

The smallest shrubs in the genus,
species which originate on windswept
mountain heights, like *Rhododendron
impeditum* may have narrow leaves
hardly more that a centimetre long.
Giants out of the rain-drenched forest
such as *R. macabeanum* can have
leaves up to almost half a metre long
and nearly half as wide, and those of
R. sinogrande are the largest of all.

The variety of shape is also great,
some rhododendron leaves being
narrow, like *griersonianum* and its
hybrid 'May Day', probably the

Autumn colour is a feature of the deciduous azaleas, most notable is *R. luteum*

The rust-red indumentum on *R. bureavii*

The upright young leaves seen with the drooping older ones on 'Loderi King George'

majority are boat-shaped or oval, and a few are quite round, for example the species *orbiculare* and *williamsianum*. Some are smooth on the upper surface, like 'Odee Wright', others such as 'Elizabeth' are rough and textured with a pattern of veins. The value of a glossy surface, in reflecting the light of the sky is seen when you look into a thicket of wild *ponticum* rhododendrons and notice how many of the individual leaves stand out from the dark effect of the whole plant because of their reflective sheen.

In leaf-colour the rhododendron genus offers a range from the light green of deciduous azaleas, through 'Britannia' and the more familiar olive greens and bottle-greens, to the darker, blue-green tones of *R. cinnabarinum*. Purply-brown is exemplified by 'Elizabeth Lockhart', and there are also greys which in certain cases appear as a solid colour, *R. lepidostylum*, and in others as a speckling of light dust over a darker ground, as with *R. yakushimanum* and many of its hybrids.

Foliage variations include variegation of course. The examples are not many perhaps but *R. ponticum* 'Variegatum', 'Goldflimmer' and 'President Roosevelt' are all worth recommending. Autumn colour is the special contribution of the deciduous azaleas, notable *R. luteum*.

Next we may look at the colour and texture of the undersides of the leaves. These can be scaly in the lepidote species, of which *R. impeditum* is our best example. They may of course be plain like *R. ponticum* or other wise they may be covered with a furry or felty hairiness called indumentum. A number of species have a brown or rust-red indumentum like *R. bureavii*, whereas that of *R. campanulatum* is orange, but paler, greyer colours also occur as in *R. macabeanum*.

Finally, there are various effects arising from the habit of growth to do with the way the leaves are carried on the plant. The most striking of these effects concern the growth of new shoots in spring. This juvenile growth is often quite different from the mature foliage and makes a fine visual contrast with it. In 'Moser's Maroon' the young growth is like beetroot, but more frequently we find lighter greens, often with red or brown scales peeling away as the shoot burst through, and in many cases the fresh leaves stand up alert among the heavier, drooping angle of the older ones. This contrast is most striking in relation to the larger leafed rhododendrons, especially 'Loderi King George'.

Preparation, planting, and aftercare

The first stage of preparation ought to be planning. Lots of people leave out the planning stage, and some don't even realise that such a thing exists! Garden design is in fact an art, which has its own experts and is of course the subject of other books. But don't be afraid of it! It only means thinking ahead as carefully as possible about what you are going to do.

Let us assume you already have ideas about the broad layout of the garden. What part can rhododendrons and azaleas play within the scheme?

This book aims to help you decide this and to choose which types are suitable for which site.

In one way, though, these plants relieve you of having to make a decision which is absolute and final. Rhododendrons and azaleas can almost be described as furniture, capable of being moved around the garden during almost any month of the year. With care and attention they can be moved even in full flower. This is primarily due to a very fibrous and compact root system. Of course, if the plants are to be moved,

you need to think as carefully about the micro-climate and soil conditions of the new position as if you were installing newly-bought ones there.

The right site for the plant

Rhododendrons and azaleas will last for many years and give continual colour and enjoyment. They will reward every effort you make to prepare the conditions thoroughly before you plant. In various gardens, I have seen many sad looking plants that were never going to make really satisfactory specimens. Most of them were only suffering because of incorrect siting or inadequate preparation of the soil.

Micro-climate

Micro-climate means the immediate climatic situation of the individual plant, which may be radically different from the conditions which obtain a mere few yards away. Unlike animals, plants cannot get up and go to a position where they would be more comfortable. Seriously, people do forget that! Siting of plants requires both care and commonsense.

Avoid definite frost pockets. These are places where freezing air is stopped in its natural tendency to pour downhill like water. It may be trapped by walls, close-set trees, dense

'Mrs G W Leak'

vegetation, or caught in a dip or hollow of the ground. Frost will not kill suitable hardy plants; nor will frost alone spoil the flowers. However, when the early blooms are hit by the direct rays of the sun with ice-crystals still on them, the sad result is always scorched brown flowers. Early-flowering rhododendrons should be placed out of reach of the early morning sun. Remember that it will be no use sheltering them with deciduous plants, which will be leafless in spring – the very time when they need shade from the south east.

The constitution of the soil

As with micro-climate, the vital characteristics of the soil can be extremely localized. Indeed they can change almost from one spadeful to the next.

Suppose just one bucketful of builders' rubble has got left on the site, and you unluckily plonk an expensive new young rhododendron in the middle of it. The plant is going to have an uncomfortable time. Clearly we need to watch out for such hazards.

The aspects of the soil's constitution that we want to look at are four; its openness/density of texture, its drainage, its humus content, and its acidity/alkalinity. In all of these respects the qualities of the soil can be favourably modified, and the ways of doing so are dealt with below. It would also be true to say that the four aspects are inter-connected but it is easiest to look at them one by one.

Root and soil texture

In the case of rhododendrons and azaleas, what we call their "rootball" is quite like a thick mat, densely formed of smallish active roots,

Good drainage is important to the success of these plants: 'Carita Inchmery'

tangled together and not reaching far underground. They are designed to take up a lot of water for transpiration through the leaves. In our subjects the leaves are generally evergreen which means they are losing a certain amount of water all year round. Because they originate mostly from regions of high rainfall, they rely on plentiful water. The roots need to be actively growing and spreading their dense mat. To do this, they require well-drained, open and rather fibrous soil. Clay is bad news for rhododendrons and azaleas and, if it is heavy, you may need to give them a special bed of different soil as described on page 42.

Soil quality problems and solutions

Heavy clay can give waterlogging problems. The lack of air within such

dense soil suppresses activity in the roots, because the micro-organisms they interact with cannot thrive. Even if your garden area as a whole has reasonable soil quality, you may nevertheless find small patches of clay left over from old excavations for foundations, septic tanks or mains pipe-trenches.

The sticky wetness and density of such soil is alleviated by improving the texture with the addition of plenty of suitable materials such as peat, leaf mould or spent hops.

Good drainage is important to the success of rhododendrons and azaleas and if your garden, or the part of it where you want these plants to grow, is very wet for months on end, they will become sad and pale, making very little growth. Many rhododendrons are shown to me with the tell-tale browning on the tips of the leaves which so often indicates a waterlogged site.

But the problem can be overcome.

'Harvest Moon' needs careful positioning and feeding but can be outstanding in May

A mixed assortment of rhododendrons and azaleas

If quite a large area is involved, the excess water can be led away by means of land drains. Of course, the proper time for the installation of these is before you begin on cultivation or planting. So you need to decide well beforehand how much trouble and expense you are prepared to undertake.

Moss growing on the soil is quite a definitive indication of bad drainage, and rushes are still worse. Dig up a lump of soil and squeeze it. If it squashes into a paste form which you can press water out, it is bad, but if it feels crumbly there are no drainage problems. If it is dusty on the other hand there may be a need to increase water-retention (which means raising the fibre content) as well as to

consider how the plants will get an adequate water supply.

Another hazard occurring in small outcrops, especially around a newly finished house is builders' rubble. This seriously degrades the soil texture for our rhododendrons, as it is hard, unfibrous and probably interrupts the natural drainage. Worst of all, any mortar and plaster it contains will create a very alkaline pH which is chemically harmful. The only satisfactory answer to rubble is to dig it up and remove it from the site.

Humus and woodland soil

The soil should contain a good amount of humus, which is the product of the natural decay of dead plants. The floor of a forest, with a

thick layer of dead and rotten leaves, is ideal, and if your garden area has actually been a woodland, it is likely to be very suitable in most respects. Improvers, which you can add to adapt less useful soil types, will be discussed under 'soil quality improvement' page 43. Mostly, these additives are simply to put in extra humus, but may at the same time give a more fibrous texture and lower the "pH".

Acidity and alkalinity – diagnosis and treatment

We still have an important geological question to consider. Where the rock below the soil is chalk or limestone, or even where the water reaching the site is exceptionally "hard", our plants may find their roots subjected

Woodland soil, full of humus, is ideal for all rhododendrons and azaleas

to a chemically alkaline environment. This will severely upset any rhododendron or azalea by disturbing its intake of iron and calcium and other elements. Ways must be found to produce more acid soil conditions, by lowering the "pH" in which alkalinity is measured.

The term "pH" is a chemist's expression for quantifying the pressure of Hydrogen ions within the solution that permeates the soil. The higher this pressure is, the more anti-acid the dissolved chemicals are. PH7 is what is scientifically called "neutral", but soil for the average garden is pH6, and the correct medium for growing rhododendrons and azaleas is ph5 or lower.

Clearly we need to know whether the problem of alkalinity exists in our garden before spending money on plants. And if there is a problem it may vary in degree in different parts of the site. Soil can change its character almost from one spadeful to the next. Even where the builders are not to blame, as mentioned above, there can be strongly localized geological differences. How shall we find out where they are, and how can we rectify them?

Professional firms can perform a soil-analysis for you, but their fees will be very expensive. You can do it quite well yourself. Then you can make sure of taking readings from each exact spot where you want to place an acid-loving plant. Kits can be bought at any good garden centre for a price you will find well justified by the long-term success of the most treasured specimens in your garden.

The operation consists of comparing a given graduated colour-scale with the colour of the solution in your test tube. The tube contains the soil sample, shaken with *distilled* water, plus the indicator-additive. Don't use tap water in these tests! It very often adds an alkalinity of its own, and gives a higher "pH" reading than if distilled water had been used. Readings of the acid/alkaline value are taken in the form of the "pH" number. This refers to the pressure of hydrogen ions dissolved in the moisture of the soil, but there is no need to go into the chemistry of it. All you need to know is that the proper value for growing our subjects is pH5 or lower. Above pH6, don't grow these plants! Between pH5 and pH6, improve the situation if you can.

Overcoming adverse conditions

If your local geology is alkaline, with chalk or limestone as the underlying rock, you cannot change this. It must be accepted that massed rhododendrons and azaleas are not destined to be the major feature of your garden, unless you move house. But you are not prevented from growing a few of them, if you are sufficiently determined to do it. You only need to provide them with a local pocket in which the soil is the way they want it. There are few ways of doing this.

Container method

If a container is used for your rhododendron to grow in, it can be filled up with soil selected for its low "pH". This can be brought in from another locality with more suitable soil. Otherwise, your local soil can have mixed into it however much moss peat, coconut fibre or fine-ground bark is necessary for the alkalinity to be overcome.

Testing, as described later, enables you to be sure that the mixture is right. If you use a container, remember that it must have good drainage holes, to save your plant from the problem of waterlogged soil.

Go for a higher site

You might think it would do some good to dig a large hole in your chalky garden, fill it generously with peat and put your rhododendron into that. This may work for a season or two, but your plant is supposed to last longer than that. After a time, the water contained in the surrounding alkaline soil, with its high "pH", will leach into the peat and make your plant unhappy after all.

A slightly different version of this approach can work, however. If an acid-soil bed for your rhododendron is formed where it is at a higher level than the surrounding limy soil, then the alkalinity will not leach upward into it. Remember only, that if the soil drainage is away from your plants you will always have to guard them against becoming too dry.

An artificial raised bed

In case you don't have a high place existing in the garden, you could make one. An edging of boards or railway sleepers, or of peat blocks can be filled up with acidic soil which then remains above the level of the chalky danger and thus safe from it. As mentioned in the previous paragraph, though, dryness needs to be prevented.

A raised bed could also be built with a dwarf wall but the mortar used in building it might become a new source of alkalinity. Anyway, to my

1 Choose a suitable container

2 Good drainage holes are necessary to avoid a waterlogged soil

3 Layer of broken stones to assist drainage

4 Container filled with soil selected for its low pH. If necessary, add moss-peat, coconut fibre or fine-ground bark to overcome alkalkinity

5 Keep top of rootball 1cm below surface level of soil.

Growing rhododendrons and azaleas in a container

mind brickwork is not a texture which easily makes an agreeable complement to the majority of rhododendrons or azaleas. Stone looks more appropriate, especially in the form of drystone walling – though it really is very dry in its drainage effect. And guess what stone you had better avoid – yes limestone!

Since a hummock of lime-free soil will remain lime-free, the obvious application is the rock garden. There, lime-hating plants can be grown on top of a whole downland of chalk. Many dwarf rhododendrons are very well-suited to this situation. Choose lime-free rocks!

Planting

Planting can really be carried on throughout the year – even, with care, when the subject is in full flower. But planting is a crucial operation for the future success of the specimen, and to achieve the very best results I would recommend doing it in the early autumn. If this is not possible, spring would be second choice. The main disadvantage of spring is the seasonal danger of dry winds and occasional drought, which can cause all evergreens to suffer, especially those recently planted.

Soil-quality improvement

Most gardens will be improved by digging in liberal quantities of moss peat, ground bark, coconut fibre, rotted bracken or leaf mould (ideally from beech or oak). Pine needles can also help to open up the soil. Any of these materials could be beneficially incorporated into the soil of the planting area.

Fertilizer – or not?

Assuming that the ground is now prepared, with sufficient humus, no lime, no waterlogging but adequate rainfall to maintain moist roots, then the plant will really require no fertilizer at all. But it can benefit at

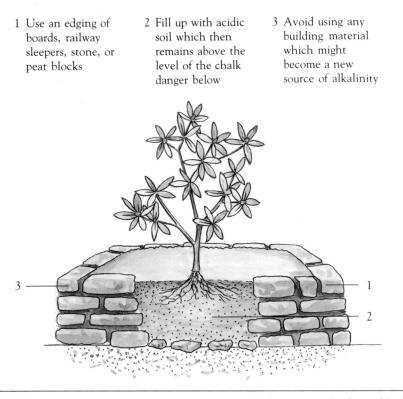

1 Use an edging of boards, railway sleepers, stone, or peat blocks

2 Fill up with acidic soil which then remains above the level of the chalk danger below

3 Avoid using any building material which might become a new source of alkalinity

Making an artificial raised bed

planting time if given a little help to become established quickly, should there be any deficiencies in your soil.

The majority of chemical fertilizers contain varying proportions of nitrogen, phosphorus and potassium compounds, usually written N, P and K respectively. Nitrogen has the effect of promoting green growth and should only be applied, and sparingly, during the spring and early summer. Phosphorous and potassium encourage healthy root-formation and ripen the woody stems of plants ready for the winter, so both are essential to healthy shrubs. If you are planting during the autumn, it will be beneficial to work well into the soil no more than 70gm per sq m (2oz per sq yd) each of superphosphate (P) and sulphate of potash (K). For spring planting you can include organic nitrogen (N) and I would recommend 70gm (2oz) per sq yd of blood, fish and bonemeal as the best source, if there might be a

deficiency.

To make all this simpler and less technical, you could apply a general purpose balanced garden fertilizer at a rate of 70gm (2oz) per square yard.

Planting procedure

Having decided the planting station, now take out a hole similar in size to the root-ball of your plant. Being fibrous-rooted, these subjects must not be planted too deeply. In fact the top of your root-ball should be only a .6– 1 cm ($^1/_4$–$^1/_2$ in) below the existing soil level. Work in your nice mixture of soil and humus around the root-ball, making sure that the roots really reach it. However, avoid pressing down too firmly, because our subjects like an open, well-aerated soil. Now water quite liberally, unless conditions have been really wet while planting. The plant will be needing extra water for transpiration at this time, and the water will also help settle the soil

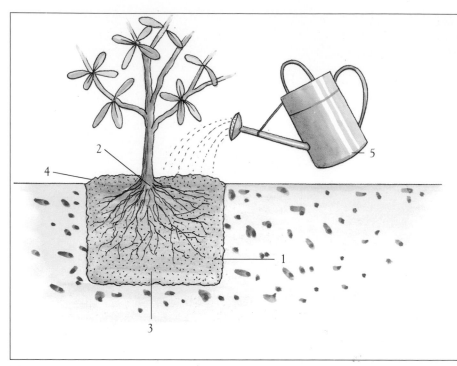

1 Dig a hole similar in size to the root-ball of your plant

2 Do not plant too deeply. The top of the root-ball should only be 1cm below the existing soil level

3 Work in soil and humus mixture around the root-ball

4 Avoid pressing down too firmly, these plants like an open, well-aerated soil

5 Water liberally

Planting

around its roots. There's much benefit, too, in putting a little mulch down around the shrub right away.

Watering after planting

See that your plants have a real good drink at regular intervals after planting if the ground is at all dry, and make sure that there is plenty of moisture in the soil throughout the year. A mere splash of water may do more harm than good, especially on a hot day. Evening is the best time to give it.

Rhododendrons and azaleas all need liberal quantities of water, especially during the growing season. Probably more plants are lost because they become dry during the late spring and summer, than from any other cause. The tell-tale sign on rhododendrons is the drooping and curling of the leaves. This is nature's way of reducing the loss of moisture from the leaves by transpiration.

During cold winter weather also, rhododendrons will hang their leaves. This, again is a drought-effect due to

the unavailability of the water which has been locked up by the frost. It is probably the drying effect of cold weather that kills plants during the winter, more often than the low temperature itself.

Water hardness

People worry a lot about giving mains water from the tap to our lime-hating subjects. It is true that tap water in England often does contain more lime than we should like, but if you have a naturally acid soil and will not be using tap water continually over many years, it is unlikely that you will see any adverse effect. However, if rainwater is available, it will be slightly acid, rather than alkaline at all, and so is ideal.

Aftercare of the soil and plant

If there is one secret for growing healthy plants, I believe it is mulching. This is the best way to create the cool, damp soil conditions which are so important to healthy growth.

Mulching consists of arranging organic, fibrous material – potential humus not fully decomposed – as a continuous layer or mat, covering the cultivated soil. The plants feed on the slowly rotting vegetation, and they also receive from its blanket effect a degree of frost-protection during the winter. Another very important advantage is that young weeds are suppressed by being hidden away from the light which they would need in order to grow.

What, when and how to mulch

Ideally your mulch should be applied in the autumn. But better another time than not at all. Without getting into the current ecological argument about its extraction, one can say that moss-peat can be used, but it is not ideal. Peat dries too much during hot weather, and once really dry is difficult to wet again. However, its use can be made more effective if a small proportion of soil is incorporated with it.

Two cautionary notes: firstly, do not use grass-cuttings. These soon rot into a wet, sticky mess and do more harm than good. Also, be careful not to use leaf mould which has been collected from alkaline woodland areas. The chalkiness is concentrated in the leaves to a surprising extent.

For very young plants, lay your mulch no more than 5–6cm (1–1.5in) thick. For more established plants this can be increased to a depth of 15cm (6in) or even 30cm (1ft). The ideal materials to use are dry bracken (my favourite) or pine needles (much used in Belgium) or leaf mould. Coarsely ground bark, hop manure and coconut-fibre are also good. Most of these latter materials can be obtained from your local garden Centre or Garden Shop.

Cultivate less, mulch more

Apart from ensuring that your plants are well watered, are free from pests and diseases, aftercare should be kept to a minimum. Avoid cultivating around your plants, because they root right on to the surface and any disturbance will do damage. If, after the first year, your plants look pale and weak, a light dressing of balanced fertilizer will do no harm. The main thing to remember is, to apply it sparingly and only when required. Healthy, established plants require no feed. But don't forget to mulch!

Pruning, if and when to do it

It is seldom necessary to prune rhododendrons and azaleas, but if the need should arise they will respond quite happily. Plants do sometimes get leggy or lopsided, or their growth may become thin and spindly. Again, they may be damaged by accidents such as tree branches falling on them, and consequently require fairly drastic reshaping. And sometimes in the case of a small garden, it is simply necessary to keep vigorous varieties within bounds.

If the need should arise for pruning, this should be carried out in early spring.

Cut back the chosen branches to just above a whorl of leaves

Pruning

Whatever pruning you find necessary should be carried out in early spring. A light pruning consists of each branch that is treated being shortened back to a whorl of leaves.

Should a more drastic pruning become necessary, many of these plants can withstand being cut back very hard, immediately after the flowering time, and should then

Rhododendrons in the wild spring garden

'Blue Danube' has been allowed to naturalise among these woodland plants

quickly break away with new growth.

A word of caution: certain particular varieties of rhododendron do not respond favourably to drastic pruning, so a certain amount of experimentation may be necessary. The best-known hardy hybrid in general use to which this applies is 'Alice'.

Dead-heading

Plants spend considerable energy in ripening their seed, and so removal of the seed capsules when newly formed will save this energy. It is surprising how much this improves growth and promote flower-formation for the following year.

This operation is really only required by your best rhododendrons, and is most important in the case of the young, recently planted specimen.

As soon as possible after flowering is finished for the year, the seedheads should be removed. Do this as shown in the sketch, being careful to break off the seedhead above the dormant bud.

Azaleas do not really require dead-heading. Sometimes one wants to remove flower-heads which are "over", simply for the sake of appearances. Even this is practicable only with the deciduous sorts of azalea. Deadheading the evergreen ones would tend to be a very long and tedious task.

Propagation

Of all aspects of gardening the propagation of your own plants is the most fascinating. How satisfying it is, to root your own cutting and watch the new plant grow and flower! Rhododendrons and azaleas offer quite a challenge to the amateur propagator and the methods by which they can be reproduced include from cuttings, by layering, by grafting and from seed.

Cuttings – taking cuttings

Many rhododendrons and azaleas can be rooted from cuttings. These can be taken when the new growth is semi-ripe, which is generally in latish summer or early autumn. Deciduous azaleas form the exception, because they yield the best cuttings from fresh, soft growth, taken in early spring.

Shoots 7.5–10cm (3–4in) long are cut, avoiding the old wood. These must consist solely of the current season's growth, and for the very best results, I suggest that you should carefully select only from young and vigorous plants.

Preparing your cuttings to root

It is good to trim off the bottom leaves of the cutting entirely, and the tips of the remaining leaves to some extent. Doing this, reduces the area from which the cutting is going to lose moisture by transpiration. The cutting cannot replace water lost in this way until its roots begin to grow.

In the case of rhododendrons, a slight wound should be made near the cut-end of the stem. This wounding, which is not necessary for azaleas, increases the area from which roots will spring. It is done by lightly scraping off the surface of the bark for the length of about an inch to expose the cambium, which is the first green layer. Then the cut end, and this wound, should be dipped into a hormone rooting compound, before being pushed into the rooting compost. Rooting compound can be purchased from your local Garden

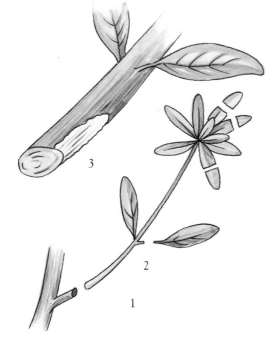

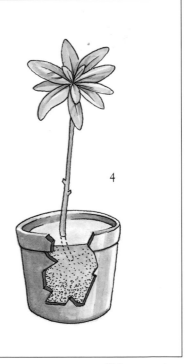

1 Choose shoots 7.5–10cm (3–4in) long. They must be of the current season's growth, and if possible only from young vigorous plants

2 Trim off bottom leaves and tips of remaining leaves

3 For rhododendrons only, make a slight wound near the cut end of the stem by scraping off the surface of the bark for about 1in

4 Dip the cut end, and the wound, into a hormone rooting powder. Insert into a mixture of 50% moss-peat and 50% sharp sand or perlite

Taking cuttings

Centre or Horticultural Shop and should be kept in an airtight container in a cool place.

Getting your cuttings to grow

When you wish to grow only a small number of cuttings, these are best placed in a seed tray with a mixture of 50% moss-peat and 50% sharp sand or perlite. Ideally the cuttings should be kept in a greenhouse and covered with a light-gauge polythene, or with the type of plastic lid which is available on many of the small plant-propagating boxes you can now buy from your Garden Centre or Horticultural Shop.

If you have in your greenhouse a small area heated with a soil-warming tray, try to keep the temperature at the base of your boxed cuttings to 21 degC (70 degF). A useful way to take an accurate soil temperature for this purpose is to fill the crack between two cutting-boxes with sand, into which you thrust the soil-thermometer.

It is advisable to let the cuttings have a breath of fresh air for about half an hour, once a week. Opening the greenhouse ventilators is probably enough, but don't forget to close them again.

Another wise precaution is to water the cuttings every ten days with a solution of a fungicide to prevent any of the fungus problems which so easily arise in a warm moist atmosphere.

Potting-on your cuttings

Many cuttings will root in eight to twelve weeks. Don't be afraid to ease one gently out here or there to see how it is progressing. Lever it free with a small split cane, and press it very gently back into the compost after inspection.

When well rooted, transfer each cutting into a small 7.5 cm (3 in) pot with a mixture of 75% moss-peat and 25% sharp sand. A little fertilizer can be added, consisting of 28g (1oz) super-phosphate, 14g ($\frac{1}{2}$oz) sulphate of potash, 14g ($\frac{1}{2}$oz) sulphate of ammonia and 14g ($\frac{1}{2}$oz) magnesium limestone. These quantities of chemical will be enough to combine with 0.03cu m (1cu ft) of potting mixture.

Be very careful with the young roots, which are delicate and can easily break off. Also, do not push the mixture down too firmly, as the plants prefer a light, open compost with plenty of air.

Keep the cuttings moist and in a warm temperature until they are really settled in and have started to make new roots in the pot. After this they can be taken outside and kept in a cold frame until they are ready to go out into your garden.

Again it is good to check on rooting progress by examining what is going on inside one or two sample pots. And it is easier at this stage because you need only tap the upturned pot gently until the contents drop out into your hand for inspection. Of course it fits neatly back into the pot again afterwards.

Remember to keep your cuttings frequently watered at every stage

Propagation by layering

This is rather a slow method of propagation, but definitely a simple one. If you are content to obtain only one or two young plants from one of your favourites, then layering may perhaps be the best way.

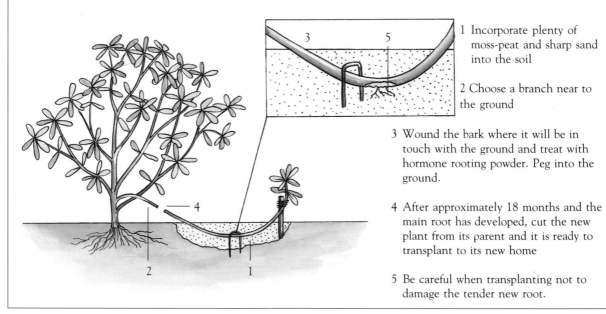

1 Incorporate plenty of moss-peat and sharp sand into the soil

2 Choose a branch near to the ground

3 Wound the bark where it will be in touch with the ground and treat with hormone rooting powder. Peg into the ground.

4 After approximately 18 months and the main root has developed, cut the new plant from its parent and it is ready to transplant to its new home

5 Be careful when transplanting not to damage the tender new root.

Propagation by layering

It is very important to incorporate plenty of moss-peat and sharp sand into the soil where you are planning to root your new plant. Choose a branch of the parent that is near enough to the ground, and peg it down as shown in the sketch. Also it is useful to wound the bark slightly, where the branch will be in good contact with the soil, and then treat the wound with a touch of hormone rooting powder. See the note about this on rooted cuttings, above.

The technique of layering can in fact be used at any time of year, but, depending upon the growing conditions which obtain when you carry it out, you may have twelve or eighteen months to wait for a well-rooted new plant. Once the necessary main root has developed, the new plant can be cut free from its parent, carefully lifted, and planted again into well-prepared soil wherever you want it. But you need to take great care, throughout this moving operation, that the tender new root does not fall off the old wood from which it has grown.

Grafting

Before we had the modern aids now used in propagation, many of our garden rhododendrons were grafted on to the stock of the "wild" *Rhododendron ponticum*. This is a way of providing a robust root system for some variety which might not grow such a strong root of its own. The drawback is that grafting often results in the troublesome development of suckers which, if ignored, may take control. One sees evidence of this in many old, neglected gardens where the original grafted-hybrid- rhododendrons have become completely overwhelmed by suckers of the more vigorous, smooth-leaved and purple-flowered *ponticum* growing up from the same roots. If you have any grafted rhododendrons, keep a sharp eye out for suckers, and carefully pull off any

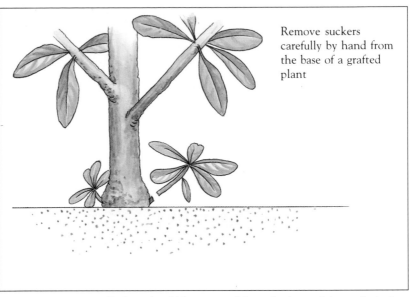

Remove suckers carefully by hand from the base of a grafted plant

Suckers should be removed from the base of the grafted plant

you find. The hybrid 'Cunningham's White' is sometimes used as an alternative grafting stock as it is less given to suckering than is species *R. ponticum*.

Despite modern aids to propagation, quite a number of rhododendron hybrids remain fairly difficult to reproduce, and sometimes the only effective way is by grafting. *R. yakushimanum* is a plant that commercial growers very generally propagate by grafting onto *R. ponticum*.

Although not many readers of this book are likely to attempt grafting, a brief description of the method may be useful to those who do so, and interesting to those who don't.

The saddle graft involves cutting converging cuts upwards into the stem of the scion. A very sharp knife indeed is required, and a turn of the blade at the top of the cut can produce a good saddle. The scion is the plant you wish to propagate, and the piece to be grafted should have a thickness of up to 6–8mm (say ⅓in). This should be bound to the stem of the root stock with raffia so as to make an intimate matching of surfaces. This should be done as soon

as the scion is prepared, which implies that the root stock has been prepared first.

The choice of the individual root stock plant requires care, especially that it should be strong, healthy and disease-free.

The root stock, cut ready for grafting has to match the scion, so it has to be chosen for the matching thickness of the stem. Before cutting, it should be showing signs of new growth, being a seedling which has been potted on into 9cm pots a few weeks before and keep in optimum conditions of moisture and warmth.

Growing from seed

Here is another slow but simple method of multiplying rhododendrons and azaleas. Simple when it works, that is! Whether it will work in a given case is a different story. Of course, the plant-breeder can only grow from seed if he means to produce a new hybrid stock by the crossing of existing forms. But hybrid plants (when they develop seed, which many do not) will not necessarily breed true to type. On the contrary, they are very likely to "throw back" to parental forms.

Since the majority of garden forms of rhododendrons and azaleas are hybrids, there is a possibility that the plant you want to reproduce may throw back or refuse to set fertile seed at all. In that event it will only be capable of propagation by the three other methods mentioned above. But there's no harm in trying.

If growing from seed is indeed what you want to try, the fat, brown seed-pods should be collected from the other plant about late December through January. Dry them off thoroughly and break them open to extract the very fine seeds, which are like flakes of tobacco. The seeds can be sown in boxes or seed pans in early spring – perhaps a little earlier if you have a heated greenhouse. A mixture of fine sifted peat is an excellent sowing medium. The seed should be sprinkled thinly on top of this, and not covered, but just gently pressed down into the surface of the peat. A sheet of glass or polythene should cover the pans. Make sure they are kept moist and warm, the ideal temperature being about 16–18 degC (60–65 degF).

Within a week or two the seed should germinate. Then the glass or polythene can be removed and the seedlings will grow away quite quickly.

When they are large enough to handle, they should be pricked out, in the same way as you would prick out bedding plants, into further boxes containing a mixture of peat with a little sand.

When they have again grown on enough they can be transferred to a small, well-sheltered nursery bed in your garden, in suitable soil, frequently watered. It is useful to keep all seedlings carefully labelled throughout the propagation project, especially if more than one breeding is in progress.

We have said nothing about how to control what pollinator fertilizes the seed. Would that not be interesting?

Tissue culture

This is a form of propagation that is becoming increasingly important for the commercial grower. In simple terms, a small slice of rhododendron tissue is placed in a test-tube which has been part filled with a special jelly or agar containing some fertilizer ingredients. The tubes are kept in bright light at controlled temperatures. These conditions encourage the small piece of rhododendron to split and produce many very small plantlets which in time can be pricked

out into trays of suitable peat compo. to make bushy young plants.

The advantages of this system ar twofold, for the grower and th eventual recipient. To be succesfull tissue-cultured, plants must be totall disease and virus free. This means tha plants derived from this method c propagation will certainly be 100% healthy when first planted, an generally grow away with considerabl vigour.

The second advantage is that enables rhododendron growers t produce very large numbers c progeny, from a promising newly developed rhododendron or azale hybrid much more quickly than woul be possible by conventional methods In these days when so much "garde news" is published, a fashionable ne cultivar can come overnight into th limelight. The commercial grower then urgently compelled, by th pressure of his own success, to suppl the market for the new plant tha everybody impatiently demands.

However, tissue culturing is ar operation requiring much technica expertise and special equipment, and so it is rather beyond the scope o most amateurs.

The white flowers of 'Palestrina' and pink flowers of 'Appleblossom'

Problems, pests and diseases

Of all plants in your garden rhododendrons and azaleas are probably still among the most disease free. However, there are a few problems and one or two insect pests which you should look out for.

Lichen

Lichen is often troublesome on azaleas, both deciduous and evergreen. Generally the cause is wet and badly-drained soil which, with lack of plant food, produces a rather stunted, slow growing plant. Deciduous varieties can be sprayed on the bark with winter wash during the dormant season. Of course, the evergreen types cannot be sprayed, and in their case the only cure is to scrub off the lichen with soap and water and a nail brush.

It is best for any old and badly-affected branches to be cut out. At the same time, you may prevent recurrence of the problem by improving the drainage and condition of your soil. Add humus to it in the form of peat, leaf mould or pine needles, plus a light dressing of balanced fertilizer in the spring.

Bark-split

This rather English hazard is a matter of being caught out by vagaries of the weather. When a hard frost occurs while the sap in running, in spring or more rarely the autumn, the bark of rhododendrons and azaleas can split badly at the base of the stem. The only defence against this is to provide temporary shelter for the plants if a dangerously unseasonable frost is forecast.

Leaf-curl

This is another effect of the weather, but not so serious as Powdery Mildew nor so likely to take you by surprise. During periods of drought, but also during very cold, frosty weather, you will notice that the leaves curl at the edge and droop from the stalk. It occurs to some extent in all our subjects, but most noticeably among the larger-leafed rhododendrons and particularly when specimens have recently been replanted. The plant is suffering from drying up and is trying to protect itself. This is nature's device to reduce the amount of moisture lost by transpiration. Looking forward to the winter, a thick mulch applied in the autumn will help to prevent leaf curl. In the case of summer drought, obviously a good drink of water will help, plus mulching.

Aphids

In certain seasons, green aphids can be a nuisance, and may attack young, fresh shoots on any of our subjects. Unless steps are taken to destroy the insects, growth will be restricted, and any new shoots which are allowed to get infested may eventually become very distorted.

Vine weevil damage on R. *sanguineum*

Keep a careful watch for these pests in spring and spray with Peremethrin or other suitable insecticide to control them if necessary.

Scale insects

These curious little creatures are mainly seen on the undersides of rhododendron leaves. Usually, the first sign of trouble is a nasty, black, sooty deposit appearing on the tops of the leaves in early summer. If you then look underneath you will see brown, limpet-like creatures about .6cm (¹/₄in) in diameter.

These will also be found on the bark. Spray them with Malathion or other suitable insecticide, making sure to spray well underneath the leaves. Then, after two or three days when the insects are dead, scrape them off with the back of a knife and wash the sooty deposit away with either warm soapy water or one of the proprietary leaf cleaner. The fungicide 'Nimrod T' can be used to remove this sooty deposit of mould.

Rhododendron flies or leaf hoppers

These are insects that attack the underside of rhododendron leaves in late spring and early summer, causing a rather mottled effect, pale-green to yellow in colour. Control this by spraying with a suitable insecticide containing Peremethrin.

Weevils

The grubs of the vine weevil, which are dirty-white in colour, may sometimes attack a rhododendron or azalea plant just below ground-level and eat all round the bark at the base of the stem. This will cause the plant suddenly to collapse and die. The gardener usually first becomes aware of the problem when the plant ought to be recommencing to grow in the spring but fails to do so properly. If such a catastrophe ever happens to your shrub, dig it up and look carefully at the base of the stem to see whether the bark has been damaged. At least this will enable you to recognise the cause, so that you can defend your remaining plants as described below.

The grubs make these forays before and after their hibernation, but unfortunately, little can be done about weevils at the grub stage. Counter-measures have to wait until they turn into adult weevils in early summer and begin to attack the leaves. They make typical small, half-moon shaped cuts as shown in the photograph. The insect is then able to be controlled by spraying or dusting with BHC (HCH) throughout the foliage and also over the surface of the surrounding soil.

This pest is now widespread throughout Britain and continental Europe, and in the USA. Research is in progress which we hope will result in the ability to defeat this very serious pest by some means of biological control.

Bud blast

This fungus disease most commonly attacks the "wild" *ponticum* rhododendron, but fortunately does not yet seem to be too serious a threat to our garden varieties.

Symptoms of this complaint are dark brown or black flower buds with black hairs on them. The affected buds fail to develop into the hoped-for spring flowers. For a small outbreak, the best response is to remove and burn the affected material, to prevent any further spread. A systemic fungicide such as benomyl (Benlate), if sprayed on to the developing buds in early spring will keep the fungus at bay. It is commonly believed that this infection is spread by leaf hoppers. If those insects should become very evident, spray them with an insecticide to gain the necessary control.

Galls

Galls afflict only evergreen azaleas and they most often appear on younger plants which are less than three years old. They are more likely to be found in a very wet season and certain azaleas such as the variety 'Rosebud', seem to be very much more susceptible to them than most. The galls themselves are ugly, wart-like growths, red or green in colour, usually first noticeable in springtime, appearing singly upon leaves, which should be picked off and burnt. The

Rhododendron leaves with powdery mildew

disease spreads by means of fungal spores which the wind and insects carry, but it seldom amounts to a serious complaint. If the plants were to become badly affected, the answer would be to spray them with Zineb.

Phytophthora

This fungus disease of rhododendrons and azaleas causes the root stem to rot. The dark leaves gradually turn pale green, then brown, and die. Unfortunately, there is very little that we can do to control this troublesome complaint. The best reaction is to remove the plant completely and burn it. Be careful not to replace it with a similar variety on or near the infected spot for a few years.

Rhododendron Powdery Mildew

This relatively new fungal problem first arrived around 1980 and has become quite a serious disease on certain rhododendrons.

Why Powdery Mildew suddenly appeared is as yet unknown. As an unpleasant newcomer it has crept up on us and often taken hold before being correctly diagnosed.

Paling of the upper leaves is the first sign of trouble. This is followed by powdery grey or brown patches under the foliage. If left untreated, some plants will gradually defoliate and eventually die.

Certain hybrids are more susceptible than others. *Rhododendron cinnabarinum* and its lovely hybrid 'Lady Chamberlain' are highly susceptible. So are some of the *griersonianum* hybrids such as the popular 'Elizabeth' and the vigorous 'Anna Rose Whitney'.

Rhododendron yakushimanum and many of its offspring have a naturally powdery appearance, especially on the young growth. This should not be mistaken for powdery mildew.

As with many forms of mildew, once it has really taken hold the powdery symptons are difficult to remove. Fortunately the sprays we use to control mildew on roses are equally effective on rhododendrons. Remember that prevention is easier than cure. If signs of the problem should appear, spray as the new growth begins, using either buprimate sold as Nimrod T, or Clobutouil sold as Systhane. This preventative spray should be repeated at four to six week intervals. One small bonus for the town dweller – you are less likely to encounter powdery mildew, due to the higher sulphur content in the air.

Rhododendrons and azaleas at Longstock Park

Page 54
A close-up of the pale cream flowers of the deciduous azalea 'Daviesii'

Plant descriptions

Listed below are 219 of the most popular and interesting rhododendron species and hybrids. (Azaleas are included as rhododendrons.) These have been grouped into six sections: tall; medium; dwarf and alpine; tender and exotic; evergreen azaleas; and deciduous azaleas.

The first table is a quick alphabetical guide that shows at a glance the page number on which you can find more detailed information about the plants. The following pages then give this detailed information. The UK Hardiness Ratings always appear after the flowering time, and wherever possible the USDA Ratings are then shown alongside. However, at the time of writing, not all USDA Ratings are available. For a complete explanation of these ratings see page 35.

Species or hybrid	Page Number	Species or hybrid	Page Number	Species or hybrid	Page Number
'Alexander'	93	'Bruce Brechtbill'	68	'Dreamland'	70
'Alice'	57	*bureavii*	68	'Dusty Miller'	84
'Alison Johnstone'	67	'Buttermint'	69	'Egret'	85
'Anna Baldsiefen'	67	*calostrotum*	83	'Elizabeth'	70
'Anna Rose Whitney'	57	*campanulatum*	58	'Elizabeth Lockhart'	70
arboreum	57	*campylogynum*	83	'Fabia'	70
'Arctic Tern'	83	'Candy'	91	'Fairweather'	71
augustinii	57	'Carita Inchmery'	58	'Fantastica'	71
'Autumn Gold'	67	'Carmen'	83	'Fascination'	94
'Baden Baden'	67	'Caroline Allbrook'	69	'Fastuosum Flore Pleno'	60
'Bagshot Ruby'	57	*catawbiense* 'Album'	58	'Fireball'	99
'Bambi'	67	*catawbiense* 'Grandiflorum'	58	'First Light'	91
barbatum	57	'Chikor'	83	'Flamenco Dancer'	91
'Bashful'	68	'Christmas Cheer'	59	'Fragrantissimum'	91
'Berryrose'	99	'Cilpinense'	84	'George Reynolds'	99
'Betty Anne Voss'	93	*cinnabarinum*	69	'Gibraltar'	100
'Betty Wormald'	57	'Coccinea Speciosa'	99	'Ginny Gee'	85
'Bijou de Ledeberg'	93	'Creamy Chiffon'	84	'Golden Torch'	71
'Blaauw's Pink'	93	'Cunningham's White'	59	'Golden Witt'	71
'Blue Danube'	93	'Curlew'	84	'Goldflimmer'	71
'Blue Diamond'	83	'Cynthia'	59	'Goldkrone'	72
'Blue Peter'	58	*dalhousiae*	91	'Goldsworth Orange'	72
'Blue Tit'	83	*davidsonianum*	69	Goldsworth Yellow'	60
'Bo Peep'	68	'Daviesii'	99	'Gomer Waterer'	60
'Bow Bells'	68	'Diamond Rosy Red'	94	'Grace Seabrook'	72
'Bric a Brac'	68	'Doncaster'	70	*griersonianum*	72
'Bride's Bouquet'	93	'Dopey'	70	'Grumpy'	73
'Britannia'	58	'Dora Amateis'	84	'Halfdan Lem'	73

Tall garden rhododendrons 2.5m upwards

'Alice'
(*griffithianum* hybrid)

May/June　　　H4　　　6b

Fast growing rhododendron with attractive pale pink flowers, best planted in a garden with plenty of space, because not happy with heavy pruning. Young plants have a definite upright habit of growth and the leaves are pointed and glossy.

'Anna Rose Whitney'
(*griersonianum* x 'Countess of Derby')

May/June　　　H5　　　6a–6b

A vigorous, fast-growing plant with dark green, rather hairy leaves and deep pink flowers that open to a rather loose truss. It grows quite quickly into a tall shrub, and can be planted as a screen. It may be susceptible to powdery mildew, for which reason I suggest it is best used on an open site.

arboreum
(species)

March/April　　　H2/4　　　7b–8a

In the foothills of the Himalayas I have seen this magnificent rhododendron living up to its name "tree like". Forests of these fine plants cover the hillsides bearing flowers of white, pale pink and scarlet shades. We have many fine old specimens of it in the rhododendron gardens of Britain too. Being a slow-growing species it will not flower very freely as a young plant. Once mature, however, it presents a spectacular pillar of bloom in early spring.

The bark on mature plants is rough and peeling, and the tough green leaves show an attractive suede brown indumentum underneath. However, the fact that a mature tree can grow to over 20ft tall tends to restrict this lovely species to the larger woodland garden.

augustinii
(species)

May　　　H3/4　　　7a–6b

Augustine Henry was a Medical Officer in the Chinese customs during the second half of the 19th century. This species, which commemorates him, is the nearest to a true blue among the Rhododendron species. It is a quickly growing plant, which flowers exceedingly freely. Specimens growing in the wild have been found to vary considerably in the colour of their funnel-shaped blooms, from rose-pink to deep violet; and the forms available in cultivation may also differ widely in their shades of blue and violet-blue. Furthermore, the flower colour on an individual plant can alter from year to year. A lightly shaded site is the most suitable for *augustinii*, though it will still grow well in the open.

'Bagshot Ruby'
(*thomsonii* x)

May　　　H5　　　5–6a

Deep wine-red flowers show up well against the tough, dark green leaves. The new spring growth on this hardy plant is also of an attractive wine-red. There are better new red hybrids now, but this old favourite is still worth planting.

barbatum
(species)

April　　　H3/4　　　7a–6b

This brilliant scarlet-flowered rhododendron may never come to be widely cultivated. Even so, I hold strong affection for it, having walked through dense forests of this lovely plant in the Himalayas. Unfortunately, it is not one of the hardiest species, but certainly worth planting where space and conditions allow. Apart from the brilliant-red flowers, this species has magnificent peeling mahogany-coloured bark.

'Betty Wormald'
('George Hardy' x)

May/June　　　H4　　　6b

A close relation of perhaps the best known of all the hardy hybrids, 'Pink

'Betty Wormald'

become a popular species with the public, it will remain a friend of mind. Flower-colour varies from lavender to blue. The foliage is attractive as the leaves are coated underneath with a lovely cinnamon indumentum.

'Carita Inchmery'
('Naomi' x *campylocarpum*)
April/May   H4   7a–6b
There are several selected clones of the Rothschild 'Carita' grex, this being one of the most outstanding. Although a tall rhododendron, it is not spreading in habit. Its biscuit-yellow, rose-tinted flowers are produced so profusely as to cover the bush down to the ground. Since it is hardy, it can be grown in a fairly open situation. Other 'Carita' forms well worth growing are 'Carita' itself, pale yellow; 'Carita Charm', pink changing to cream, and 'Carita Golden Dream', cream and pink, changing to white.

catawbiense 'Album'
(selected seedling)
May/June   H4   5
This is the albino or white-flowered form of the Catawba Rhododendron, which flowers profusely and is especially good as an informal hedge, or screen. Like many other kinds of shrub, it will work best as a flowering hedge if the flowers are allowed to remain, and are not clipped off with the close trimming given to a formal hedge.

catawbiense 'Grandiflorum'
(selected clone)
May/June   H4   5
The Catawba river in North Carolina gave its name to the species of which this plant is a named clone. Its chief merit is an extreme degree of hardiness, which tolerates even the sub-zero temperatures of Scandinavia. This makes it a popular garden plant throughout Northern Europe. In

Pearl', but not quite so vigorous. Even so it will eventually require plenty of space. Its large cone-shaped trusses of pink flowers appear late in the spring flowering season.

'Blue Peter'
(*ponticum* hybrid)
May   H4   5–6a
If a bold splash of blue is wanted in the garden in late spring, this is the plant to provide it. Its frilly, trumpet-shaped flowers are blue, ringed with violet, paling towards the red-spotted throat. It flowers freely, sometimes lasting into June, and is strong and upright in habit.

'Britannia'
('Queen Wilhelmina' x 'Stanley Davies')
May   H4   6b–6a
This is no longer seen as one of the most popular hybrid rhododendrons. In spite of its patriotic name, 'Britannia' is a Dutch introduction, over 50 years old. It grows slowly to form a compact, rounded plant, which is tough and wind-resistant. The glowing, deep-red flowers are thickly clustered against a background of distinctive pale-green leaves, which are quite unlike any other rhododendron in their colouring.

campanulatum
(species)
April/May   H4   6b
In the Himalayas, between ten and fourteen thousand feet, I have walked through gnarled forests of *Rhododendron campanulatum*. The hillsides glowed lavender-blue from the massed flowers. The effect was unforgettable and so, even though this may never

'Christmas Cheer'

'Christmas Cheer'
(*caucasicum* hybrid)

February	H4	5–6a

The normal flowering time for this hybrid is February, but in a mild winter, or a sheltered garden, it will unfold its pink buds in January. The colour of the fully open flower is white. It used to be customary to force this subject so that it would bloom at Christmas, whence the name; and it is a very good plant from which to cut shoots, just when the buds are unfolding, and bring into the house for extra-early flowering. As with all these early kinds, the flowers are liable to be damaged by frost. This dense, compact bush, will grow well in a light or slightly-shaded place, and will bloom when still quite small.

'Cunningham's White'
(*caucasicum* x *ponticum* 'Album')

May/June	H5	5

Hardy, fast growing and tolerant of conditions that would be too alkaline for the majority of rhododendrons. These are a few of the plus points for this old hardy hybrid. Pale lavender buds open to white flowers with deep-yellow freckles in the throat. Not an exciting plant, but it does have a definite value when planted as a screen or hedge. Very easy to root from cuttings.

'Cynthia'
(*catawbiense* hybrid)

May/June	H5	5

This old hardy hybrid has been very popular, and will grow surprisingly fast under ideal conditions. Excellent as a tall, hardy evergreen to fill a gap or form a screen. But beware, because it may grow up to attain a final height of 20ft (7m). It would therefore be unwise to choose this hybrid for a small garden! The trusses of up to 24 deep pink flowers are large and conical. It is an easy rhododendron to root from cuttings.

Britain it is less often grown, perhaps because it quite resembles the ubiquitous *ponticum* with its lilac-purple flowers in May and early June. Given time, it will grow into a large shrub about 4.5m (15ft) tall.

'Cynthia'

'Goldsworth Yellow'

'Fastuosum Flore Pleno'
(*catawbiense* x *ponticum*)
June   H5   5

Originating in Belgium almost a hundred and fifty years ago, this well known hybrid has been very widely planted. Around many gardens in Britain, during late May or early June, you will spot the distinctive double, blue flowers produced on a rather loose flower-truss. Bushes over 7m (20ft) high are not uncommon, which means that a large garden is the proper home for this plant. It is easy to root from cuttings.

'Goldsworth Yellow'
('Jacksonii' x *campylocarpum*)
April/May   H4   5b

This is one of the oldest of yellow hybrid rhododendrons, having been grown since at least 1925. Even after being propagated for so long, it remains a strong and hardy plant, flowering at the end of April or in early May. The funnel-shaped flowers are apricot coloured in bud, but open to pale yellow, speckled brown in the throat. There may be as many as 16 in a truss. The bush is dome-shaped, rising eventually to about 5m (17ft) high, and will grow in the sun, as well as in shade.

'Gomer Waterer'
(*catawbiense* hybrid)
May/June   H5   5

This tough old hybrid is guaranteed to withstand the most extreme weather conditions. Its large, tough, dark-green leaves are very distinctive. The large flowers are white with a lavender flush. It will generally flower late in the spring, lasting even into early summer.

'Hawk Crest'
(*wardii* x 'Lady Bessborough')
May   H3   7

This remarkable rhododendron, one of Lionel de Rothschild's hybrids from his garden at Exbury, first flowered in 1950. Though still fairly scarce, it is very well worth growing. 'Hawk Crest' forms a rather open, loose plant which will do more than justice to a lightly wooded position. The buds are deep orange, changing to lemon-yellow as they unfold, and each flower-truss contains about a dozen blooms, held erect. The result is a magnificent spectacle.

'Lionel's Triumph'
(*lacteum* x 'Naomi')
early May   H4/5   6a–6b

Named for the late Lionel de Rothschild but not until the lost clone was rediscovered after his death. This is one of the many excellent hybrids that he raised at Exbury, in Hampshire. Its bold trusses of creamy-yellow flowers show red markings in the throat. The plant eventually forms a sturdy, open bush with dark green

'Gomer Waterer'

'Fastuosum Flore Pleno'

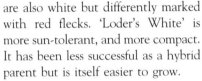

'Lionel's Triumph'

…eaves, but is not an easy one to …row, and very difficult to root.

'Loderi King George'

(*griffithianum* x *fortunei*)

May   H3   7a–6b

'Loderi' is perhaps the most important hybrid rhododendron every produced. It gave rise to numerous different named clones, of which this is the best, and certainly lives up to its imperial name. 'King George' has enormous trusses of funnel-shaped, sweetly scented, flowers which are pink in bud, unfolding to white, with green markings in the base of the throat.

'Loder's White'

(*?arboreum* 'Album' x *griffithianum*)

May   H3   6b

Eighty years old and still popular, this large, white-flowered hybrid remains uncertain about its parentage. It should not be confused with the later 'Loderi King George'. Both are scented, this one less so. Its flowers are also white but differently marked with red flecks. 'Loder's White' is more sun-tolerant, and more compact. It has been less successful as a hybrid parent but is itself easier to grow.

macabeanum

(species)

April/May   H5   7a–6b

You will need plenty of space and, ideally, woodland conditions to grow this lovely rhododendron species from northern India. The flowers are pale lemon-yellow with deep-red markings which appear early in the season. Long shiny leaves give interest all the year round and silver candles of new growth in the spring add a spectacular early display. Under ideal conditions this plant will grow into a tree of over 10m (30ft).

'Madame Masson'

(*catawbiense* x *ponticum*)

May/June   H5   5

Like the other hybrids produced from the same two parent species, it is a useful, tough plant that will withstand the most extreme conditions. One of the best to form a strong hedge or screen. The flowers are white with faint yellow markings and appear late in spring to early summer. Easy to root from cuttings.

'Mrs Furnival'

R. macabeanum

'Moser's Maroon'

May   H4   6b

One of the criticisms made of rhododendrons is that they have one glorious burst of colour in late spring, and then subside into mediocrity for the rest of the year. 'Moser's Maroon', a French hybrid, escapes this castigation as it has bright distinctive red bark on all the new growth, and the young leaves are fiery copper-red, only fading in autumn. The deep maroon-red flowers, black-spotted, provide a striking combination with the young growth throughout May, and the total effect is quite remarkable. Tall and vigorous, the plant will grow moderately quickly to its ultimate height.

'Mrs Furnival'

(*griffithianum* x *caucasicum*)

May/June   H4   6b–6a

Famous as a hybrid of 1920 vintage, 'Mrs Furnival' is a slow-growing plant.

Once established, it puts on only a few inches a year, so its habit is compact and dense. The flowers are softly pink, funnel-shaped, blotched with wine in the throat, and gathered in a tightly-packed trusses. This is a well-tried and reliable plant which would not overwhelm a small garden.

'Mrs G W Leak'

('Coombe Royal' x 'Chevalier Felix de Sauvage')

May/June   H4   6b–6a

Unusually coloured flowers make this Dutch hybrid rhododendron stand out among the crowd. They are large, open, funnel-shaped, and rosy pink, with a conspicuous black to dark brown blotch in the throat which catches the eye at once.

'Naomi'

('Aurora' x *fortunei*)

May   H4/5   6b–6a

On a warm spring evening, the scent from 'Naomi' is simply exquisite. This is one of the most successful of Lionel de Rothschild's hybrids and was named after his daughter Naomi. The rather open flower heads glow with mixture of pink and yellow. Some of the older specimens at Exbury are now over 20ft high, forming rather open bushes with distinctive rounded greygreen leaves. Sadly this subject is quite prone to powdery mildew.

'Naomi Exbury'

('Aurora' x *fortunei*)

May   H4   6b–6a

The Rothschild's famous garden at Exbury has been the nursery of very many first-class rhododendron hybrids. 'Naomi Exbury' is one of the best, being a form of 'Naomi', which is itself a wonderful rhododendron. It is quite a large plant, clothed in grey-green leaves which give it a curiously clean-cut appearance. Large fragrant, wide-open flowers, in pastel lilac-pink, tinted pale yellow, unfold from cerise-crimson buds.

'Naomi Glow'

('Aurora x *fortunei*)

May   H4   6b–6a

The 'Naomi' grex is remarkable for its fragrant flowers, so large and wide-open. The clone 'Naomi Glow' has blooms of sparkling pink, with

'Mrs G W Leak'

R. oreotrophes

brown markings in the throat. This fine hybrid has an open habit and its foliage is more grey than green. The leaves, besides providing just the right foil for the flowers, ensure that the plant is more ornamental out of flower than most rhododendrons.

oreotrephes
(species)
April/May   H4   6b
The Tibetan and Burmese mountains are the home of this rhododendron species, which forms a large shrub. It flowers profusely and varies a great deal from form to form in the colour of its flowers, which range from pale mauve with brownishcrimson spots, through shades of lavender-pink to deep rosy-lilac. The leaves also vary in shape from long to round, and have an attractive bloom on them. It is not generally described as deciduous, but in cold gardens it does lose its foliage in winter. Even so, it is very well worth growing, being highly ornamental.

'Pink Pearl'
('George Hardy' x 'Broughtonii')
Apr/May   H4   6b
'Pink Pearl' is a hybrid rhododendron which first caught the public's fancy nearly a century ago, so that it is probably found in more gardens than any other hybrid. It is undoubtedly very pretty when in bloom with its large, delicately lilac-to-pink flowers

fading to white at the edges. It is a strong and quite fast-growing plant which seems to be happiest in woodland. Its drawback is a tendency to become rather bare and gaunt-looking at its main stem. As it ages, groundcover plants around it, such as *Cornus canadensis*, *Erythronium* and species *Cyclamen*, would help to conceal the ugliness of the sparse growth of its lower part.

ponticum
(species)
May/June   H5   6b
Ponticum has become naturalized to such an extent in Britain that it is often regarded as a native plant, even a weed. However, the name is taken from 'Mare Ponticum', the Latin name for the Black Sea, and it does in fact grow wild in Asia Minor, Armenia and the Caucasus, also in the Balkans, Spain, and Portugal. It was introduced

'Pink Pearl'

'Purple Splendour'

to England from Gibraltar in 1763 and the British climate suited it perfectly. *R. ponticum* has now escaped from cultivation to become one of the most distinctive evergreen shrubs in our landscape.

Formal hedges of this shrub are dense and evergreen, and withstand regular clipping with equanimity. Informal hedges, allowed to flower and not clipped closely, are especially attractive. It is also excellent as a shelter-belt, as it grows to between 3–6m (10–20ft).

If it were not so common, we should have to admit that *ponticum* has a lot to commend it as a flowering shrub. Flowering in May and June, and varying in colour from pale lilac-pink to mauve depending on the clone. The banks of these shrubs which have become naturalized in many woodlands present a splendid spectacle when in full bloom. This species should not be despised, simply because it is so easily grown.

ponticum 'Variegatum'
(Cloned selection)

May/June	H4	6b

This variety, with leaves irregularly marked in creamy-white on the margins, is much less vigorous and invasive than the 'wild' rhododendron species in its plain-leaved form, and its flowers are a pale lavender. It is especially popular with flower-arranging enthusiasts. Its height can eventually reach about 6m (20ft), but it can be restricted without harm, making a much smaller plant.

'Purple Splendour'
(*ponticum* hybrid)

May/June	H4	6b–5/6a

As against the pinks, red, oranges and yellows which commonly occur in rhododendron hybrids, a true purple is unusual. This one has the genuine imperial purple for its flower colour, emphasized with a prominent black ray in the throat. Besides this, it flowers profusely and rather late, particularly if grown under a light covering of trees. Its upright habit is reminiscent of its parent, *R. ponticum*, but its moderate height makes it a practical plant for the smaller garden.

'Sappho'
(Waterer hybrid of unrevealed parentage)

May	H4	5

Quite startling flowers, pure white, show in the throat a pronounced rich-purple blotch, overlaid with black. In late May or early June, the dome-shaped trusses carry fifteen blooms or more, funnel-shaped and up to 7cm (3in) wide. This is one of the old hybrids introduced by Waterer's Nursery about 1867, at a time when hybridizing programmes were jealously guarded secrets, as explained in my historical chapter. 'Sappho' will grow to about 4.5m (15ft) with a tendency to spread. Pruning is therefore usually necessary when mature, to contain its growth and to keep it flowers.

sinogrande
(species)

April	H3–4	7b/8a–7a

In 1912 the famous plant collector, George Forrest, was staggered to come across a rhododendron species growing in the forests of Burma and Tibet which had leaves 90cm (3ft) long, and 30cm (1ft) wide. The altitude at which he found these plants was 3,000–4,200m (10–14,000ft) where they varied in size from large shrubs to trees of 9m (30ft) or more in height. Given shelter from wind and plenty of moisture, they make magnificent plants for the large garden or woodland. The flower trusses are large, containing at least twenty flowers, which are bell-shaped and creamy white with a crimson blotch in the throat. There is a northern form which has softly-yellow flowers. Out of flower, the huge leaves will always be a talking point, especially as they have a silver-grey, or biscuit coloured indumentum on the undersurface.

'Susan'
(campanulatum x fortunei)

May   H5   5–6a

Fairly late in the flowering season, 'Susan' stands out as a cool, blue-flowering rhododendron with excellent foliage and attractive, soft-brown indumentum under the leaves. It will grow into a large, spreading bush and therefore requires plenty of space.

thomsonii
(species)

April   H3   7a

Perhaps this lovely species from the high Himalayas is a rhododendron for the real enthusiast. It has many attractive features, including distinctive round leaves, glaucous green in colour, and peeling red-brown bark which, with a smooth stem below, gives all year round interest. Open, bell-shaped flowers in a rich blood-red colour complete the beauty of this plant. *R. thomsonii* is certainly not often planted and may be expensive or difficult to obtain.

'Virginia Richards'
('Mrs Betty Robertson' x)

May   H5   6b–6a

An interesting hybrid that will always attract attention. The flowers combine pink with apricot-cream and have a very distinctive red eye in the centre. The plant grows quite quickly into a neat bush but sadly it is prone to powdery mildew. If this problem can be overcome it will certainly gain popularity.

yunnanense
(species)

May   H4   7a–6b

This appealing rhododendron species, which is ideal for woodland planting, appears to be covered in a mass of delicate pink or mauve butterflies all through May. The flower colour, which can vary a great deal from form to form, may be white, pale pink, rose pink, rose-lavender or lavender. It has the fortunate ability to grow in sun or shade, though a little shade is preferred.

'Susan'

'Alice'

Medium garden rhododendrons 1–2.5m high

'Alison Johnstone'
(*yunnanense* x *concatenans*)

May	H4	6b

Attractive trusses of bell-shaped flowers fading to soft pink from pale orange. These show up well against the grey-green foliage. Sadly susceptible to powdery mildew. If this should arise, spray as instructed.

'Anna Baldsiefen'
('Pioneer' selfed)

Mar/April	H4	6b

An outstanding low-growing rhododendron that is often among the earliest and gives a magnificent display of bright pink flowers. An upright neat bush, ideal for the smaller garden.

'Autumn Gold'
(*discolor* x 'Fabia')

May/June	H5	5

Lovely apricot-salmon flowers with a deep orange eye in the centre. A useful hybrid from the USA that gives colour late in the flowering season. It can be rather shy to flower as a young plant.

'Baden Baden'
('Essex Scarlet' x *forrestii* Repens)

April/May	H5	5

This strong, compact hybrid was raised in Germany and therefore bred to withstand very low temperatures. Excellent for the smaller garden and able to survive on an exposed site, it eventually forms quite a dense bush about 1–1.3m (3–4ft) high. The tough, leathery leaves have a distinctive curl. It will start to bloom as quite a small plant, with deep-red waxy bell-shaped flowers.

'Bambi'
(*yakushimanum* x 'Fabia Tangerine')

May	H5	5

A compact dome shape of grey-green foliage dusted with silver indumentum gives this rhododendron interest all the year round. An old specimen in my own garden, now 3ft high, is covered in a mass of orange-pink

'Alison Johnstone'

'Bashful'

flowers every year. This is an excellent *yakushimanum* hybrid that enjoys growing in full sun.

'Bashful'
(*yakushimanum* x 'Doncaster')
May   H5   6a
Large rose-coloured flowers fading to off-white, plus silvery foliage make this an attractive *yakushimanum* hybrid for the small garden, even if not the most exciting of them all. It is easy to grow and hardy.

'Bo Peep'
(*lutescens* x *moupinense*)
March/April   H4   6b
Early flowering and easily damaged by spring frost, this straggly grower with yellow-green flowers has been superseded by many better, similar coloured plants. However, it has remained an old friend with me, bravely displaying its flowers while the snow is still on the ground.

'Bow Bells'
('Corona' x *williamsianum*)
May   H4   6b
'Bow Bells' has R. *williamsianum* as one parent which accounts for the bell-shaped flowers. These are cerise coloured while still in bud, but unfold to a soft and charming pink. The young shoots which appear at the same time, are coppery bronze, so that the whole plant is unusually colourful in spring. The rounded leaves clothe a nicely compact bush which fits very easily into a small garden. It is still not out of place in a larger setting, if used as a group planting.

'Bric a Brac'
(*leucaspis* x *moupinense*)
February/March   H4   6b
There is charming plant of 'Bric a Brac' flowering now in my conservatory, and I'm writing in mid-February. It looks very graceful, with white flowers attractively edged in pink. In the garden it also flowers very early in the year and is sadly subject to spring frost. Plant this in a specially sheltered site unless you live in a very mild climate. It is easy to root from cuttings and an excellent subject for the cool glasshouse or conservatory.

'Bruce Brechtbill'
('Unique' sport)
April/May   H4   6b
Attractive foliage covered in a light dusting of silver indumentum. This is a sport of the old favourite 'Unique' and has inherited the same compact habit of growth. The flowers are pink, edged with yellow.

bureavii
(species)
April/May   H4   6b–6a
This Chinese species grows in the province of Yunnan at an altitude of 3,900m (13,000ft). It has rose-pink, bell-shaped flowers, marked with

'Bow Bells'

'Bambi'

crimson, and the further merit of foliage which has a thick, bright rusty-red, felty indumentum on the undersurface, very attractive in winter sunshine. The stems of the young growths also have a coat of this woolly felt, varying from pale fawn to bright rust in colour.

'Buttermint'

('Unique' x 'Fabia')
May   H4   6b
Recently introduced, with handsome yellow flowers are flushed with pink, and compact growth. I am dubious about the foliage of this variety which appears to mark rather badly.

'Caroline Allbrook'

(*yakushimanum* x 'Purple Splendour')
May/June   H5   6–6a
Purple flowers are not usually popular, perhaps because they remind us of the wild species *R. ponticum*. I must admit there are more exciting colours, but this is a useful hardy, compact plant.

cinnabarinum

(species)
April/May   H3/4   6b–7a
Certainly one of the most distinctive rhododendron species. Remarkable flowers of wax-like bells that vary in colour from red to deep orange and through to yellow. The neat, round leaves are of an attractive glaucous green which forms an exciting contrast with the flower-colour. Under ideal conditions *R. cinnabarinum* will form a tall shrub, 3–4m (10–12ft) high. The lovely red-flowered var. *roylei* is one of my favourite forms within this species, and the soft-orange subspecies *concatenans* is another.

Sadly the recent scourge of powdery mildew has attacked this species with a vengeance. I have seen large plants totally defoliated by the disease, although other varieties nearby remained completely clean.

davidsonianum

(species)
April/May   H3/4   6b–7a
Another Chinese Rhododendron species. This one, which was sent back to Britain in 1908 by the plant collector, E H Wilson, has a rather open habit. Its unusually narrow, dark green leaves are the backing for flowers which vary considerably in colour from form to form. Purplish-rose, pink, pale rose or white may occur, as well as shades in between, and the flowers may also be marked with reddish spots. All its forms are

'Baden Baden'

'Dreamland'

completely hardy, but one of the best pink ones has received an Award of Merit, so if you are buying a *davidsonianum*, I recommend that you specify the pink-flowered kind.

'Doncaster'
(*arboreum* x)

| May | H5 | 6b |

A widely-planted old hardy hybrid, raised in Holland. A free-flowering plant whose deep red flowers have dark spots in the throats. It eventually grows into quite a big bush that is best suited to the larger garden.

'Dopey'
(Hybrid from 'Fabia')

| May | H4 | 6b |

This is a reliable plant which will not take up too much space. It is of medium height with a slightly upright habit of growth and large intensely red flowers.

'Dreamland'
(Hybrid combining 'Fabia', *discolour* and *yakushimanum* ancestry)

| May | H4 | 6b |

Attractive ice-pink flowers on a neat, compact bush. This is an excellent *yakushimanum* hybrid and probably the best of all pale pinks.

'Elizabeth'
(*forrestii* Repens x *griersonianum*)

| April | H4 | 6b |

'Elizabeth' is undoubtedly one of the outstanding low-compact rhododendron hybrids. It will grow slowly to about 1.25m (4ft) tall, reaching its ultimate height only after many years. 'Elizabeth' produces a mass of blood-red, rather waxy, trumpet-shaped flowers, each at least 7.5cm (3in) wide. The leaves are an unusual soft green. A prostrate form of this plant exists, called 'Jenny' or sometimes 'Creeping Jenny', whose flowers are longer, bigger and a lighter red. It is also a little earlier flowering.

'Elizabeth Lockhart'
(sport of Hummingbird)

| April | H4 | 6b |

A really lovely plant when grown under ideal conditions. The shiny leaves are a rich maroon-red, giving interest all the year round. Rich deep red flowers in April glow against the lovely foliage. Plant this preferably in light shade, to preserve the lovely leaf-colour.

'Fabia'
(*dichroanthum* x *griersonianum*)

| May/June | H4 | 7a–6b |

Prolific in flowering, 'Fabia' has a rather squat habit, forming a spreading rather than an upright bush. In early summer, trusses of funnel-shaped flowers unfold, of an orange to salmon colour backed by greyish green leaves of exactly the right tone to set off the blooms to perfection. Being completely hardy, it is a first-class plant for any garden, especially as it helps to prolong the flowering season.

'Fairweather'

May   H4   6b

Travelling along the west coast of America, I stopped at a small nursery and there was my namesake. Unfortunately not the most outstanding rhododendron, but it has flowered for the first time in my garden this year. It appears to be compact and quite slow growing.

'Fantastica'

('Mars' x *yakushimanum* hybrid)

May   H5   5

On a recent visit to Belgium, I suddenly spotted this outstanding frilled two-tone flower. With its petals edged in deep pink, shading to very pale pink inside, it certainly presents a striking appearance. This a fairly-new, hardy *yakushimanum* hybrid raised in Germany, and I am sure it will live up to the name 'Fantastica'.

'Golden Torch'

('Bambi' x *griersonianum*)

May   H4   6b

This is unusual among dwarf hybrids of *yakushimanum* stock, in that it has a flower-colour approaching yellow. Really the name could give rise to some confusion as the flowers are certainly not golden. Soft pink buds open into quite a large deep-cream flower with a flush of pink. As the blooms fade, they turn to creamy white. It is a compact grower with good foliage and well suited to the smaller garden.

'Golden Witt'

(*dichroanthum* hybrid)

April/May   H4   6b

A fairly recent introduction from America, unusual for the red spots seen in the primrose-yellow flower,

'Fabia'

this compact, sun-tolerant plant may prove to be a useful newcomer when it becomes more familiar and more readily available.

'Goldflimmer'

(probably *ponticum* 'Variegatum' x *catawbiense*)

May   H5   5

Attractive green-and-gold variegated foliage makes this quite an eye-catching new variety recently raised in Germany. It appears to be a compact plant, superior in strength and habit of growth to the other variegated rhododendrons that are available to date. Unfortunately, the purple flowers, similar in colour to the species *ponticum*, are a big disappointment.

'Elizabeth Lockhart'

'Elizabeth'

'Goldkrone'
(hybrid with *wardii* parentage)

May   H4

An excellent free-flowering yellow rhododendron producing large trusses of funnel-shaped flowers over a long period. It forms a neat, round bush, ideal for the small garden.

'Goldsworth Orange'
(*dichroanthum* hybrid)

May/June   H4   6b

Raised in 1938 at Slocock's Goldsworth Nursery, this rhododendron has achieved its popularity largely by virtue of its name. Really, it is flying under false colours and could not properly be called orange. Salmon-pink is the best word to describe the colour of the flowers, which appear in fairly lax trusses.

'Grace Seabrook'
('Jean Marie de Montague' x *strigillosum*)

April/May   H4   6b

This is a recent arrival from America which promises to be quite outstanding among the bright-red rhododendrons of fairly compact habit. It has the added bonus of handsome foliage, which gives it a bright future as a desirable plant for gardens large or small.

griersonianum
(species)

June   H3   7b

Rather prone to frost-damage, mainly due to making a late flush of growth in the autumn, this is an untidy plant with a somewhat lax habit of growth.

'Fantastica'

'Grumpy'

season and remain well into June. *R. griersonianum* has proved extremely fruitful as a parent, producing hybrids such as 'Elizabeth', 'Fabia' and 'Vanessa Pastel', and this species is very easy to root from cuttings.

'Grumpy'
(*yakushimanum* x)
May   H4/5   6a
This is useful hybrid from the species *yakushimanum* forming a very compact plant with interesting foliage. Flowers are cream-coloured, with some orange markings in the throat. Fairly easy to root from cuttings.

'Halfdan Lem'
('Jean Marie de Montague' x 'Red Loderi')
May   H4   6b
The distracting designation of this interesting rhododendron commemorates the name of a notable hybridizer from the American north west coast. The flowers are brilliant

However, it responds well to fairly severe pruning. The bright scarlet flowers appear late in the flowering

scarlet-red with distinctive red anthers. I have seen only small specimens in flower, but have heard that this plant may develop a rather untidy habit of growth.

'Helene Schiffner'
(*arboreum* hybrid)
May   H4/5   6a–6b
An old hybrid raised in Germany, it is one of the most startlingly white rhododendrons. Ebony buds opening to flowers formed in tight round trusses. The flower shape is inherited from its parent *arboreum*. Slow growing but still one of the best pure-white hybrids. Its usefulness in California and South Australia depends upon its resistance to heat and direct sunshine.

'Hoppy'
(*yakushimanum* x 'Doncaster')
May   H5   5–6a
One of the many hybrids from the

'Halfdan Lem'

'Hotei'

grower on the American west coast, I suddenly spotted this outstanding flower among a whole batch of others. The blooms on Lem's Cameo are large, with the unusual shades of pink, apricot and pale yellow, and in the base of the flower is a deep-red eye. The colour combination is highly dramatic. Unfortunately the plant is fickle as well as beautiful, and a sheltered site plus a great deal of attention is required for it to succeed.

lutescens
(species)

February/April   H3   7a–6b

A beautiful, early flowering rhododendron. Its new growth in the spring has an attractive, bronzy-red colour, and the foliage gives another excellent show of colour in the autumn. The delicate, pale-yellow flowers, with long elegant stamens, appear at any time from February to April, covering the whole bush in a mass of blossoms. As it is early-flowering, *lutescens* requires a sheltered position.

'Markeeta's Prize'
('Loderi Venus' x 'Anna')

May   H4   6b

Bold, scarlet-red flower trusses which glow against the dark-green foliage augur a great future for this excellent new hybrid from America.

'May Day'
(*haemotodes* x *griersonianum*)

May/June   H3   7a

This is another hybrid which should be better known that it is. It flowers late, producing startling, brilliant-red, wax-like blooms, backed by grey-blue leaves apparently sprinkled with white powder. 'May Day' really is a very special plant which does not grow large, although is somewhat spreading.

'Moonstone'
(*campylocarpum* x *williamsianum*)

April/May   H3   7a

This is rather a rainbow of a plant.

famous Waterers' Nursery at Bagshot, this is yet another excellent medium-sized rhododendron for the small garden, a very hardy plant that will grow happily in full sun. Very free-flowering, with attractive, frilled, pink flowers that fade with age to white.

'Hotei'
(Goldsworth Orange' x *wardii* hybrid)

May   H4   6b

Perhaps one of the best deep-yellow flowers on any fairly hardy rhododendron. I have always found 'Hotei' quite slow-growing, and rather shy to set flower-bud until quite mature. This may be a cause of frustration for the hasty gardener, but the patient one is rewarded because the colour is outstanding.

'Humming Bird'
(*haematodes* x *williamsianum*)

April/May   H4   (7a)–6b

This neat compact bush carries very dark-green foliage shading to almost bronze, and attractive, loose trusses of deep-red, rather waxy flowers. It is an easy rhododendron to grow and

easy to root from cuttings but I have found it reluctant to flower in its early years.

'Hydon Dawn'
(*yakushimanum* x 'Springbok')

May   H5   5

This compact, free-flowering *yakushimanum* hybrid has attractive light-pink frilled flowers. The dark, glossy foliage is dusted with warm whitish tomentum.

'Jean Marie de Montague'
(*griffithianum* hybrid)

May   H4   6b

During my last visit to Oregon, on the west coast of America, this old bright-scarlet hybrid was putting on a marvellous display in towns and gardens. It is also suitable for Australia, but not for north-east Europe. While not fully hardy, it is an excellent, tough, early plant with a fine red flower truss.

'Lem's Cameo'
('Dido' x 'Anna')

April/May   H3–4   6b–7a

Visiting a well known rhododendron

'Morgenrot'

'Lem's Cameo'

'Humming Bird'

'Helene Schiffner'

'Odee Wright'

moupinense
(species)
January/March   H3/4   6b–7?
A charming species from Szechwan
in western China. The flower-colour
of *moupinense* ranges from white to
delightful deep-pink form. Being one
of the first rhododendrons to flower
in the year, it is tender and can suffer
severe frost damage. However, if you
have a mild climate or a very
sheltered spot in the garden it is well
worth trying.

mucronulatum
(species)
February   H4   6b
Winter flowers are always welcome
aren't they? In Britain the blooms of
this species appear in the first weeks
of the New Year. They are completely
frost-resistant and are a bright
rosy-purple colour, with a funnel
shape. Most unusually among
rhododendrons, this one is deciduous.
Occasionally the new growth is
damaged by frost, but the plant repairs
this later in the season. If
mucronulatum is planted in association
with the golden-flowered Witch-
hazel, *Hamamelis mollis*, the winter
garden will be immeasurably cheered.

Its rounded, bright-green leaves are
attractive at any time, and they are
enhanced by the delicate creamy-
yellow, bell-shaped, nodding flowers,
edged with pink, which unfold from
brown-red buds. The plant is
dome-shaped, not tall, and would be
a decided asset in any garden.

'Morgenrot' ('Morning Red')
(*yakushimanum* x 'Spitfire')
May/June   H5   6b
Raised in the cold climate of
Germany, this is a robust, compact
rhododendron. Its good foliage, plus
an abundance of rose-red flowers,
make this a worthwhile plant for all
gardens. It will root from cuttings
quite easily.

'Nancy Evans'

R. *orbiculare*

orbiculare
(species)
April   H4   6b
Almost round, grey-green leaves make this quite a distinctive species. The flowers are rose-pink and shaped like small bells. Certainly well worth including in any rhododendron collection.

'Paprika Spiced'
('Hotei' x 'Tropicana')
April   H4   6b
A dramatic flower which combines a wide range of colour through red to orange, with distinct red markings in the throat. However, this plant is somewhat a poor grower, and I have found the foliage can look rather pale and sickly. I really wonder if it will prove to be satisfactory in the garden.

'Percy Wiseman'
(*yakushimanum* x 'Fabia Tangerine')
May   H4/5   6b–a
Many of the *yakushimanum* hybrids could be deprecated for their similarity of colour. 'Percy Wiseman' makes an interesting colour break with attractive, two-tone flowers of pale yellow with a peach-pink flush. It is certainly one of the best, being also easy to grow and easy to root from cuttings.

'Pink Cherub'
(*yakushimanum* x 'Doncaster')
May   H5   6a
Among the *yakushimanum* hybrids this one shows quite an upright habit of growth. The foliage has a positively silvery sheen, which sets off the attractive, rose-pink blooms. It is quite free flowering.

'Praecox'
(*ciliatum* x *dauricum*)
February/March   H4   6b–6a
This hybrid is a 'must' for every garden! It is deservedly popular, being extremely pretty, early-flowering, and

'Nancy Evans'
('Hotei' x 'Lem's Cameo')
May   H3/4   7a–6b
Definitely an exciting newcomer from the USA. Last spring, 'Nancy Evans' flowered for the first time in my own garden producing large hose-in-hose flower-trusses with a combination of yellow inside the flower and deep orange outside. Good foliage and a dense habit of growth will certainly make this a popular plant that should succeed when placed in a sheltered site.

'Odee Wright'
('Idealist' x 'Mrs Betty Robertson')
May   H4   6b
The glossy green foliage is enough to make this a noteworthy rhododendron. Add to this, lovely creamy-yellow flowers, and you have an outstanding plant. When the buds first break they are rich apricot, and the open yellow flowers still have a soft apricot tint. The habit is compact, so this is definitely one of the best medium growers for large or small gardens.

'Percy Wiseman'

'Praecox'

R. pseudochrysanthum

'Pink Cherub'

...mall. The plant, which will be no more than 2m (6ft) high after many years, bears its funnel-shaped, translucent, rosy-lilac blooms during February to March in Britain. A sheltered position is advisable for 'Praecox', to protect the flowers from frost.

'President Roosevelt'

(a Belgian *arboreum* hybrid)

May   H4   6b

It is quite a mystery why this hybrid is not more popular and better known. The combination of really exciting foliage, which is ideal for flower-arranging, with beautiful flowers must be unique. Yet in spite of being cultivated for many years, this Belgian hybrid has never achieved the popularity which it so well deserves. The dark green leaves are splashed with gold in various shades, and the equally beautiful flowers are white in the centre, shading to pale pink and finally to red at the frilled edges, like a picotee carnation. To achieve the most marked leaf-colour variegation, this plant should grow in the open, not in the shade.

pseudochrysanthum

(species)

April/May   H4–5   6b–6a

This outstanding rhododendron from Taiwan deserves to be more popular. The silver-grey foliage alone makes it well worth planting, and its assets include delightful flowers, mainly white with a touch of pink. In full flower, it is a truly wonderful sight. *R. pseudochrysanthum* is available in various clones, of which my favourite is the Exbury form because of its superior foliage. An open site is best for this plant.

'Quaver'

(*leucaspis* x *sulfureum*)

March/April   H3   7a

The parents of this charming little hybrid are both small, with a tendency to early flowering. Clusters of pale-yellow blooms will appear in a mild spring, but, sadly, it is not completely hardy. In fact it should not be planted except in warm, sheltered gardens, because not only may the flowers be browned by frost, but the plant itself might be checked or even killed.

quinquefolium

(species Azalea)

April/May   H4   6b

This azalea species forms quite a twiggy shrub. It can be difficult to establish, and needs cosseting in its youth. However, it is well worth the trouble for the sake of its large, delicate, bell-like flowers which are startlingly pure white, green spotted, and 5cm (2in) wide. The young leaves also are attractive in spring with a red-brown edging, and again later in autumn when they change from green to orange and red.

racemosum

(species)

April   H4   7a–6b

R. racemosum is one of the best of the neater species rhododendrons, and it more than deserves its Award of Garden Merit. Height varies a good deal from a few inches to 1.8m (6ft), and flower colour also varies from rose pink to pale pink, or even white. *R. racemosum* has the habit, unusual in rhododendrons, of flowering all along the stems, instead of at the shoot tips only. This characteristic, together with its elegant grey-green leaves, makes it a particularly pretty plant. Flowering time is generally April. Interplanting with heathers produces one of the best visual effects in the garden. It is easily grown from seed.

'Rothenburg'

(*williamsianum* x 'Diane')

April/May   H4   6b

Large, creamy-white, funnel-shaped flowers are produced on this plant, very beautiful in their own right, but the foliage that sets them off is just as exciting all the year round, being bright apple-green and glossy. In spring, the new leaves unfold to reveal the surfaces so polished and brightly shining that they seem to have been painted with clear varnish.

russatum

(species)

May   H4   6b–5/6a

This very variable species, being a twiggy plant with slightly bronze foliage, reminds me of the thickets of low-growing dwarf rhododendrons that cover the high open hills of the Himalayas. More than most species, it presents many different forms, ranging in flower-colour from deep purple to pale pink. It is only worthwhile to grow the best clones, such as the FCC Selection from Exbury, which displays intense purple blooms.

'Scintillation'

(*fortunei* x)

May   H5   5

An excellent hardy hybrid, raised for growing on the cold east coast of North America, this is a tough vigorous plant that will tolerate the most extreme conditions. The large leathery leaves and open habit give the impression of a sturdy, well-built shrub. The large pink flowers have distinctive brown markings in the throat.

'September Song'

('Purple Splendour' x *dichroanthum*)

May   H4   6b–6a

A fairly new rhododendron from the USA which flowered in my garden for the first time in 1991. It certainly has an unusual and exciting colour which I would describe as translucent deep orange: a really lovely flower on a rhododendron that will surely become very popular.

'September Song'

'Seta'
(*spinuliferum* x *moupinense*)

March   H3   6b

An interesting plant but early flower-ing, which sadly means that in many districts it will be susceptible to spring frost. It should only be tried outdoors in sheltered, mild gardens. Perhaps it is best regarded as another interesting candidate for the cool conservatory. Its unusual, tubular flowers are pink with a dark stripe down the side. It is rather straggly when young, because rather fast-growing, but in time makes a well rounded bush. Easy to root from cuttings.

'Seven Stars'
('Loderi Sir Joseph Hooker' x *yakushi-manum*)

May/June   H4–5   6b

'Seven Stars' is a comparatively new hybrid, raised at Windsor Great Park, and given an Award in 1967. It has potentially a very good future, though it is still rather difficult to obtain. Vigorous, and strongly growing, it flowers freely and reliably, with bell-shaped blooms. These are white with a pink flush and frilly edges, opening from buds which are red to deep-pink.

'Souvenir of W C Slocock'
(*campylocarpum* hybrid)

May/June   H4   6b

The Slocock nursery is one of those in Britain specializing in growing and breeding rhododendrons. This hybrid, named after one of the family, is a first-class plant, vigorous and densely habited, with a medium height when fully grown. In early summer, its pale orange-pink buds unfold to exquisite bell-shaped flowers, softly coloured in pale yellow, flushed apricot and pink. It is a choice plant for any garden, and completely hardy.

'Surrey Heath'
(Hybrid with 'Fabia' x *yakushimanum* parentage)

May   H5

The silver-grey foliage, with a whitish tomentum on top of the young leaves attractively shows off the deep-pink flowers with a creamy-yellow centre. This free flowering hybrid is certainly a popular one.

'Taurus'
('Jean Marie de Montague' x *strigillosum*)

May   H4   6b

An outstanding introduction for the USA, It is a vigorous grower with excellent glossy green foliage and rich red trusses of flower. Attractive red flower-buds add interest during the winter months. This will definitely become a very popular rhododendron when more widely available.

'Teddy Bear'
April/May   H4   6b

With the species *bureavii* as a parent this new introduction has inherited the lovely brown indumentum under the leaves giving all year round interest. Creamy white flowers

'Temple Belle'
(*orbiculare* x *williamsianum*)

April   H4   6b

It would be difficult to find a more

'Seven Stars'

'Scintillation'

appropriate name for this plant. Both its parents come from China, it is exceptionally pretty and the flower shape could be described in no other way. The pale rose-pink bell flowers hang downwards in clusters of three or four. The grey-green leaves, heart-shaped and rounded, cover the plant to ground level, forming an attractive mound of foliage all the year. The shelter of light woodland will enable it to grow to perfection.

'Tessa'
('Praecox' x *moupinense*)
February/March   H4   6b–6a
Dear 'Tessa'! Every year this is one of the brave rhododendrons that tries to brighten my garden in late February, but so many times its bold display is ruined by frost. In a mild season the whole bush is covered with a mass of purple-pink flowers. There is also an interesting white form of this plant which flowers happily in my conservatory. It is easy to grow and to root from cuttings but does need a frost-free climate or a sheltered position.

'Titian Beauty'
(*yakushimanum* x 'Fabia Tangerine')
May   H4   6b
Interesting dark-green leaves with a light sprinkling of dusty brown

indumentum below. The flowers are waxy and red. This is not quite as hardy as some *yakushimanum* hybrids, and the leaves can become scorched in cold windy conditions, so it is best planted in a sheltered part of the garden.

'Trewithen Orange'
('Fullhouse' x *concatenans*)
May   H4   7a-6b
A delightful plant with very pale orange, waxy flowers that hang like long bells. The foliage is an attractive grey-green in colour. Unfortunately, this lovely plant, raised at Trewithen Gardens in Cornwall, is very prone to powdery mildew. However, a plant in my garden, which I sprayed with the fungicide Nimrod T, appears to be mildew-free. It is a lovely rhododendron which I should be sad to be without.

'Unique'
(*campylocarpum* hybrid)
April   H4   6b
The name of this hybrid is appropriate since no other plant shares its strange flower colour. The colouration seems to defy exact description, being given by various authors as 'biscuit-yellow', 'ochre flushed apricot', 'creamy-white tinted pink', 'ochre tinged peach' or 'flesh changing to buff'. The bush on

which these distinctive flowers are found is compact and very handsome.

'Vanessa Pastel'
('Soulbut' x *griersonianum*)
May   H4   6b–7a
An excellent free-flowering hybrid to adorn the milder garden. Among long, narrow leaves it displays attractive creamy flowers, with a strong pink flush and darker markings inside. It roots easily from cuttings.

'Viscy'
('Diane' x *viscidifolium*)
May   H5   5
The name of this hybrid is a pun between its parentage and the whisky colour of its blooms. The flowers are certainly an unusual shade of orange-brown giving this rhododendron an unique appearance. It forms an open, sturdy plant with large, leathery dark-green leaves.

'Wally Miller'
(*yakushimanum* x 'Glamour')
May   H5   5–6a
Many years ago visiting the famous Isabella Plantations in Richmond Park, I spotted this quite outstanding rhododendron in flower. It returned with me to Exbury Gardens and was named after the Head Gardener at Isabella – Wally Miller. A profusion

'Tessa'

'Unique'

'Winsome'
('Humming Bird' x *griersonianum*)

May	H4	6

This excellent rhododendron is we
suited to the smaller garden, havin
quite a dense habit of growth
especially when planted in the oper
The grey-green foliage is attractive
unfolding from bronzy new shoots
The red buds open to deep-pin
flowers, and 'Winsome' produce
plenty of bloom even as a youn
plant. It is quite fast-growing, an
roots very easily from cuttings.

'Yellow Hammer'
(*sulfureum* x *flavidum*)

April/May	H4	6

This is a somewhat unusual rhodo
dendron which will certainly no
appeal to everyone. The small yellow
tube-like flowers seen in the sprin
quite often reappear in the autumn
It forms a rather upright, straggl
bush with tiny narrow leaves, and
fairly hard pruning is essential to
keep it in shape. Quite easy to roo
from cuttings.

of pale pink flowers and attractive silver foliage make this one of the best Yakushimanum hybrids.

'Wilgen's Ruby'
('Britannia' x 'John Walter')

June	H5	5

An old and reliable hardy hybrid that is still grown on a large scale, especially for use in the colder parts of Europe. 'Wilgen's Ruby' has rich, red flowers and excellent foliage on a compact plant keep this rhododendron popular for every sort of garden. It is quite easy to root from cuttings.

'Winsome'

Dwarf and alpine rhododendrons

'Arctic Tern'

(*trichostomum* x)

May/June   H5   5–6a

A newcomer to the world of rhododendrons might suppose that this charming plant belonged to quite a different family. Its small tight little bunches of white flowers resemble those of a Daphne. This is a hardy plant that is easy to root and flowers late in the spring, and should become a very popular dwarf rhododendron.

'Blue Diamond'

('Intrifast' x *augustinii*)

April   H4   6b–6a

'Blue Diamond' really does have blue flowers. In April the plant apparently turns completely blue as the flowers unfold. The effect is remarkably attractive. It is a small slow-growing rhododendron, compact and rounded in habit. The rock garden, the front of a mixed border or a patio container are all good sites. The small, grey-green leaves have a pleasant, aromatic smell when crushed.

'Blue Tit'

(*impeditum* x *augustinii*)

April   H4   6b

A compact and fairly slow-growing plant that flowers freely in an open position, it is suitable for any small garden, and also for rock gardens. 'Blue Tit' produces a mass of funnel-shaped flowers which are borne in clusters at the ends of the branches.

calostrotum

(species)

May   H4   6a–6b

It is sad that some of the best of the charming dwarf species are not more appreciated and planted. The name 'calostrotum' means 'with a beautiful covering', which aptly describes the way its mass of rose-crimson flowers show up against the silver foliage. Originating in the high lands of Upper Burma and South West China, this plant is best grown in an open, well-drained site. If possible, select the very excellent FCC form 'Gigha'.

campylogynum

(species)

April   H3–4   7a–6b

A really charming dwarf rhododendron, with perky little flowers like small red bonnets that are held on delicate stalks away from the plant. As with many species, the flower-colour of R. *campylogynum* is variable, ranging from shades of purple to red, pink and even white. Low-growing clones such as Myrtilloides are an ideal choice for the rock garden, but be sure to keep the soil moist enough for them during dry summer weather.

'Carmen'

(a form of *sanguineum* x *forrestii* Repens)

Apr/May   H4   6b

This superb dwarf rhododendron, almost prostrate in habit, has waxy, bell-shaped flowers of a deep-red colour appearing in spring. 'Carmen' is ideally suited for a small garden or rockery, being generally not more than twelve inches high when fully grown.

'Chikor'

(*chryseum* x *ludlowii*)

May   H4   6b

An attractive yellow-flowering dwarf that sadly can be quite difficult to cultivate. The hot dry summers we have experienced have not suited 'Chikor'. Cool, moist soil with plenty of humus are really its main requirements. It forms a twiggy little

'Carmen'

'Cilpinense'

bush with small, round leaves. Its quite open, pale-yellow flowers have some attractive spots in the throat.

'Cilpinense'
(*ciliatum* x *moupinense*)
March   H4   7a–6b
When this hybrid was introduced in 1927 it immediately obtained an award. 'Cilpinense' is not very big, and forms a rounded bush on which large bell-shaped flowers are produced. The average size of the flowers is 6cm (2.5in) wide and they are freely produced, so the bush becomes startlingly attractive when the white and pink-tinted petals of the open flowers are seen with the deeper pink buds mixed among them. Because it flowers early, it is often caught by spring frost, so it is best planted in the shelter of a large tree or shrub.

'Creamy Chiffon'

'Creamy Chiffon'
(Bred in North West USA from undisclosed parentage)
May   H4   6b
This is one of the very few double-flowered rhododendrons and has orange flower buds opening to creamy-yellow blooms. It forms a dense, compact plant with good dark foliage, and should become a very popular choice.

'Curlew'
(*ludlowii* x *fletcheranum*)
April/May   H4   6b
One of the many excellent dwarf rhododendrons raised by Peter Cox at Glendoick in Scotland. The foliage on 'Curlew' has a shiny, bright-green fresh appearance. The yellow-green flowers are surprisingly large, and open wide to cover the bush in a mass of colour. Also the little red dots in the base of each flower add to the attraction of this lovely dwarf when you look at it closely. An excellent plant for any garden, small or large.

'Dora Amateis'
(*carolinianum* hybrid)
April/May   H5   5
Raised in America, where it is deservedly very popular, this hybrid is a winner: an easy to grow, free-flowering dwarf which will no doubt be very widely adopted in Britain. The attractive, pointed pink buds open to cover the whole bush in a mass of white flowers which show occasional pink markings. Planted as a small group, this dwarf rhododendron will make a lovely picture in the spring. As an added bonus, it is very easy to root from cuttings.

'Dusty Miller'
(*yakushimanum* hybrid)
May   H4   6b
The silver foliage is the most outstanding feature of this compact

'Curlew'

compact and very free flowering. The massed small flowers are so thick they often cover all the foliage. Interesting shades of pink to white give this excellent dwarf rhododendron an unusual two-tone effect. It appears to be happy planted in sun or shade. An easy one to root.

impeditum
(species)

April/May   H4   5–6a

The enormous variation in size amongst rhododendrons is not generally appreciated. They can range from tiny, creeping shrublets to trees of 9m (30ft) tall and more. *R. impeditum* is one of the smallest, only a few centimetres high, and presents a tangle of branchlets, clothed in tiny blue-green leaves less than 2cm (1in) long. Equally small mauve or purplish-blue open flowers cover the plant. It comes from high up in the mountains of the Yunnan province of China and accordingly should be given the most exposed position possible – preferably on a rock garden.

keiskei
(species)

April/May   H5   5–6a

Without doubt the most popular form is var. *cordifolia* 'Yaku Fairy'. The name certainly has appeal. It forms a low growing mat of twigs and is

plant, giving interest all the year round. It has a distinctive, neat, low-growing habit. The flowers are pink, fading to cream.

'Egret'
(*campylogynum* 'White' x *racemosum* 'White Lace')

May   H4   6b

This really charming dwarf rhododendron is a definite favourite of mine. I was introduced to it a few years ago on a visit to a meeting of the American Rhododendron Society. There it was displayed in a bed of rhododendrons set up in a shopping mall. To my surprise I found it was just one more of the excellent dwarfs raised by Peter Cox at Glendoick. Plant this little treasure in a sunny open position and you will be rewarded with a display of lovely small white bell-shaped flowers which contrast well with the dark green

shiny leaves. An easy one to root from cuttings.

'Ginny Gee'
(*keiskei* 'Yaku Fairy' x *racemosum*)

April/May   H5   5–6a

A fairly new and quite outstanding hybrid raised in America, tough,

'Dora Amateis'

'Egret'

covered in a profusion of pale yellow flowers in the spring.

keleticum
(species)

Apr/May   H5   6b–5/6a

If you consider growing dwarf rhododendrons for ground-cover, this ground-hugging plant will certainly be a candidate for your choice, with its flat and creeping habit. *R. keleticum* has open, crimson-purple flowers which cover the plant in late spring or early summer.

'Lori Eichelser'
(Parentage not yet published)

April   H4   6b

Recently introduced, this dwarf makes an interesting new addition. 'Lori Eischelser' has deep-red bell-like flowers form a loose open truss. Quite free flowering, even on young plants. Very dark green foliage. Easy to root from cuttings.

'Patty Bee'
(*keiskei* 'Yaku Fairy' x *fletcheranum*)

April   H5   5–6a

One of the very best dwarf yellow rhododendrons raised to date. Attractive glossy green foliage on a compact plant. The mass of pale yellow blooms appears early in the season. 'Patty Bee' flowers very freely,

is easy to grow and to root from cuttings. Definitely a plant to be included in any collection of rhododendrons.

'Peeping Tom'
(*wardii* x 'Mrs Furnival')

April/May   H5   5

Here we have a very attractive, blotched white flower presented on a compact bush, making this new rhododendron virtually unique. The nearest equivalent has been 'Sappho', which offers similar flowers, but has a poor, straggly habit of growth. An excellent introduction.

pemakoense
(species)

Mar/April   H4   6b

This charming dwarf and spreading species was collected in Tibet by the renowned plant hunter, Frank Kingdon Ward. Coming from such mountainous country, it is hardly surprising that it requires an open site. It has a very early flowering season, so the buds and flowers are often ruined by spring frost. This sadly excludes *pemakoense* from usefulness in really cold gardens.

'PJM'
(*carolinianum* x *daurieum*)

March   H5   5

A fairly fast-growing plant with an upright habit. Leaves turn an attractive bronze colour in the late autumn and winter. This is a very tough, early flowering rhododendron suitable for really cold sites. The flowers which are rosy purple, appear early in the season but have the advantage of withstanding some frost. Best planted in an open site, PJM is easy to grow and roots readily from cuttings.

'Pink Drift'
(*calostrotum* x *polycladum*)

April/May   H5   5

'Lori Eischesler'

'Peeping Tom'

A low, twiggy bush with small grey leaves and small purple-pink flowers early in the season. There are definitely better dwarf rhododendrons, but 'Pink Drift' is still widely available and popular. It is a tough, free-flowering plant that is happy in an open position and easy to root from cuttings.

'Princess Anne'
(*hanceanum* Nanum x *keiskei*)
April   H4   6b
This really charming new dwarf hybrid rhododendron is ideally suited to the small garden. 'Princess Anne' forms a dense, low-growing shrub, which is covered in a mass of pale yellow flowers during April and May, with foliage bronze when young. Unfortunately, this plant is in short supply at the time of writing, but the situation may improve.

'Ptarmigan'
(*microleucum* x *leucaspis*)
March   H4   6b
A delightful dwarf rhododendron that I really enjoy. It is a low spreading plant with attractive, small, dark-green leaves, very free flowering with a mass of pure white small flowers which have very distinctive black-tipped stamens. Sadly, it does flower early in the season, and so can be ruined by spring frost, to avoid which, it could be grown as an interesting cool greenhouse or conservatory plant. Outdoors, 'Ptarmigan' prefers to be planted in an open site and it's ideal for the larger rock garden. Easy to grow and root from cuttings.

'Ramapo'
(*fastigiatum* x *carolinianum*)
April/May   H5   5
One of the really tough rhododendrons which can survive under the most extreme conditions. The flowers are violet-blue and appear freely on the low, compact bush. The foliage is an attractive blue-grey colour, giving interest all the year round. Easy to root from cuttings.

'Razorbill'
(*spinuliferum* x)
April   H4   6b
This dwarf rhododendron really is unique. Its flowers take the form of pink tubes in a tightly clustered truss, and give this excellent plant a remarkable appearance. It is quite hardy, with a compact habit.

'Patty Bee'

'Sapphire'

('Blue Tit' x *impeditum*)

April   H4   6b

This is a good little plant for the rock garden, covering itself in open funnels of lavender-blue, each centred with a mass of long delicate stamens. The small grey-green leaves are barely visible during flowering, but make the plant attractive at other times. Its form is a hummock of equal height and width.

'Sarled'

(*sargentianum* x *trichostomum*)

May   H4   6b

I am sure many people would find it

'PJM'

difficult to identify this as a rhododendron. The dense, low plant with very small leaves bears charming clusters of white flowers that could easily be mistaken for Daphne. The diversity of the rhododendron family is well illustrated in this delightful plant, which is easy to grow and to root from cuttings.

'Scarlet Wonder'

('Essex Scarlet' x *forrestii* Repens)

May   H5   5

Raised in Germany, with the ability to withstand the most extreme cold, this must be one of the most widely-planted of all rhododendrons. Its brilliant, scarlet-red, rather frilly trusses of bloom show up well against the dark red foliage. The deep red flower buds make a show throughout the winter that is also very attractive. Easy to grow and to root from cuttings.

'Shamrock'

(*keiskei* x *hanceum* 'Wanum')

April   H5   5

An excellent, compact plant with pale, yellow-green flowers. Whose good foliage has a faint bronze tinge. In my garden, 'Shamrock' flowered about two. weeks earlier than the

fairly similar rhododendron 'Princess Anne'. These two excellent dwarfs can give colour from early April well into May.

'Snow Lady'

(*leucaspis* x *ciliatum*)

March   H3–4   6b–7a

This is an easy, very free-flowering rhododendron from the USA that often forms flower bud when only a few centimetres high. It has attractive, rather hairy green foliage and single pure white flowers with distinctive dark stamens. It blooms early and therefore needs shelter from cold wind and frost, but is easy to root from cuttings.

'Teal'

(*campylogynum* white x *luteiflorum*)

May   H4   6b

Many of the dwarf yellow rhododendrons have a low spreading habit. 'Teal' is definitely an exception growing upright to around 60–95cm (2–3ft). Excellent foliage and attractive yellow flowers. Easy to root from cuttings.

'Wee Bee'

(*campylogynum* 'Patricia' x *keiskei* 'Yaku Fairy')

April/May   H5   5–6a

This delightful little plant is very compact, growing to a maximum of 2ft. It has flowered for me the first time this year, producing charming little flowers with a marked frill, which combine a mixture of pink and cream colouration.

'Wigeon'

(*minus* Carolinianum x *calostrotum* 'Gigha')

May   H5   5

The grey-green foliage gives interest all the year round. During April and May, a mass of deep-pink flowers shows up against the light background. This is an easy plant to root from cuttings.

'Scarlet Wonder'

'Yaku Princess'

'Ptarmigan'

'Shamrock'

R. *yakushimanum*

R. *williamsianum*

williamsianum
(species)

April/May   H4–5   6a–6b

Among the most charming small species, this rhododendron has many points in its favour. The bush, best planted in the open, is neat and dome-shaped with interesting, small round leaves. The new spring foliage is a lovely shade of copper, often appearing with the first flowers, which are delightful pink bell-shaped blooms, grouped in loose clusters. R. *williamsianum* is fairly slow-growing, and ought to be protected from the late spring frost which can ruin the lovely young growth and brown the flower. However, it is quite easy to root from cuttings.

'Yaku Princess'
('King Tut' x *yakushimanum*)

May   H5   5

Very similar to the parent species *yakushimanum*, this is a very hardy plant with excellent deep greeny foliage with suede brown indumentum, and bold round trusses of pink and white flowers.

yakushimanum
(species)

May   H4   5–6a

This species is the most outstanding of all semi-dwarf rhododendrons and should be included in all gardens, large or small, that can grow the ericaceous plants. Found growing wild only on the island of Yakushima, off Japan, this magnificent rhododendron was introduced at Exbury by Lionel de Rothschild in 1934. Its ultimate height of 1.2m (4ft) is reached only slowly, and mostly it is seen as a low-growing and spreading, dome-shaped shrub. The narrow dark green leaves set off the flowers which are starkly white when they are open, though deep pink in bud. When in flower, towards the end of May, the whole plant can be completely covered with blossom. The new leaves in spring have a silvery covering, but the undersides of all the foliage has a velvety brown indumentum. Altogether, *yakushimanum* is a really beautiful rhododendron throughout the year.

Tender and exotic rhododendrons for the conservatory and indoors

Many plants are described elsewhere in this chapter in relation to their role as garden plants, but are as suitable or better in the greenhouse or conservatory. Among these are *Rhododendron* 'Bric a Brac' (p68), 'Cilpinense' (p84), 'Egret' (p85), *moupinense* (p76), 'Ptarmigan' (p87), 'Tessa' (p81), and Japanese Azaleas 'Bijou de Lederberg (p93), 'Blaauw's Pink' (p93), 'Hino Crimson' (p94), 'Hinomayo' (p95), and 'Mother's Day' (p95).

'Candy'
May/June   H1
then September
Vigorous fast growing vireya with a more compact habit of growth than many in this series. Soft pink slightly scented flowers.

dalhousiae
(species)
March/April/May H2/3   7b–8a–7b
I should like to see the whole family of tender rhododendrons grown more widely than they are. To thrive outside they require very mild conditions, but in my opinion these lovely subjects make really excellent pot plants for the cool frost-free glasshouse or conservatory. If they have a fault, perhaps it is their rather straggly habit of growth, which requires regular

pruning. I usually do this soon after flowering. The lovely cream-coloured flowers of *R. dalhousiae* are out in my conservatory early each spring, filling the whole building with their perfume. Many of the tender rhododendrons do have an exquisite scent, and nearly all of them root easily from cuttings.

R. dalhousiae 'Rhabdotum' is a distinctive variant, having a bold red stripe down the side of each flower. It is described in the RHS handbook as a separate subspecies within *R. maddenii*.

'First Light'
July/September   H1
This is definitely one of the easier vireyas. It is free-flowering and quite

compact in habit. It has charming pale-pink flowers.

'Flamenco Dancer'
May/June   H1
then September
Yellow-apricot flowers appear on this plant continually through the late spring and summer. A very vigorous vireya with bright shiny leaves.

'Fragrantissimum'
(*edgeworthii* x *formosum*)
March/April/May H2   7b–8a
The name indicates the chief claim to fame of this hybrid, which is perhaps the most widely-grown of all tender rhododendrons for the conservatory. White flowers, with a

R. dalhousiae

'Java Light'

tinge of pink, open early under conservatory or glasshouse conditions and they are indeed very sweetly scented. It does unfortunately suffer the common fault of so many tender rhododendrons, which is straggly growth, so keep it carefully pruned or train it against the conservatory wall. Easy to root from cuttings.

indicum
(species)

This species also referred to as Azalea Indica, provides in its different forms and cultivars, those many and various, pretty and highly-coloured pot plants that are widely available in England at the Christmas season. The plants in this range are not identified or named as hybrids, but simply sold by their colour, because they are really regarded as living decoration. It is possible to treat them as plants, to keep them going and bring them back into flower. But if you want satisfaction from the use of your green fingers, other subjects will be more rewarding. These Indicas were at their best the moment you bought them.

'Java Light'
July/September   H1

As the name suggests, this is a vireya rhododendron, hybridized from Indonesian parents, and it has a more open, upright habit of growth than most of the others. It is a vigorous plant with good foliage and the flowers are quite spectacular. The lovely pointed buds open to clusters

of brilliant orange flowers. In my conservatory, it blooms from late summer until early autumn.

'Lady Alice Fitzwilliam'
(*edgeworthii* hybrid)
March   H2   7b–8a

In really mild districts, this rhododendron can survive outdoors. However, personally I prefer to use 'Lady Alice' as a conservatory pot-plant, and have some splendid specimens that put on a wonderful show early in the spring. It is able to form quite a neat bush, unlike some of its more disorderly relatives.

'Sesterianum'
March/April   H1

A tender plant this is only suitable for the conservatory or very mild gardens. Attractive, highly scented white flowers with a light pink flush and appealing rather glaucous foliage. Easy to root from cuttings.

'Simbu Sunset'
July/October   H1

This is one of the first vireya rhododendrons to show colour in early summer, with repeat flowering into the Autumn. It flowers very freely, with pale orange blooms, but pruning is required to keep the plant compact and bushy.

'Thai Gold'
May/June   H1
then September

A really beautiful vireya that will surely become popular as a cool conservatory plant. In common with many members of this exciting group of rhododendrons, I find that 'Thai Gold' will flower in the late spring and again in the early autumn. A mass of rich yellow blooms completely cover the bush with a dramatic display of colour. It forms a compact bush that responds well to pruning, and, as with the majority of vireyas, it is easy to root from semi-ripe cuttings.

'Sesterianum'

Evergreen azaleas for the garden, patio and conservatory

'Alexander'
May/June   H4

A strongly trailing habit obviously makes this an excellent azalea for planting in a tub or hanging basket. Small orange flowers cover the dangling stems late in the spring.

'Betty Anne Voss'
May   H4

An interesting double pink flower, very similar to 'Rosebud', but this plant appears to be the stronger grower of the two. However, it remains a compact azalea that will eventually become broader than tall.

'Bijou de Ledeberg'
April   H3

I have found this an interesting azalea, being one of the new evergreens with variegated foliage and rose-red flower. It grows happily in a pot, to flower March/April in a cool conservatory, but outdoors it is suitable only for a mild situation, as it is somewhat tender.

'Blaauw's Pink'
April/May   H4

This rather upright small shrub was bred at Boskoop, Holland, in the late 19th century. It was one of the earliest European-made hybrids in this Kurume group of Azaleas, based on stock originating from the Japanese island of Kyushu. While most types have a single flower, certain hybrids have double ones, so formed that one flower seems to be set inside another, in the same way that some of the old-fashioned primulas are. We call this 'hose-in-hose'. 'Blaauw's Pink' has such flowers, of a salmon-pink colour.

'Blue Danube'
June   H4

A most distinctive and unusual hybrid, whose flowers are a deep blue-violet, appearing late. Their size is large for an evergreen azalea, up to 7.5cm (3in) wide. This is one of the Vuyk Hybrids, a group which appeared soon after the First World War from the Vuyk van Nes Nursery in Holland.

'Bride's Bouquet'
May   H3

On a visit to the west coast of America, I saw this azalea growing splendidly in many small gardens. Its charming, double white flowers show a hint of green in the centre. This beautiful plant requires a sheltered site to achieve the best results. Alternatively it makes an excellent subject for the cool conservatory.

'Betty Anne Voss'

'Diamond Rosy Red'

'Diamond Rosy Red'
May/June   H5

I first spotted this whole range of Diamond Azaleas growing on a nursery in Belgium. The neat, compact habit was very apparent. These tight little bushes are covered in late spring with a mass of tiny blooms; rosy-red in this case. Other Diamond Azaleas are available with lilac, pink or white flowers. This series of hybrids, raised in Germany to withstand the extremes of European weather, will be a welcome addition in gardens that experience severe winter conditions.

'Fascination'
May   H3

A really dramatic azalea, certainly worth trying in a really mild garden but which sadly is not too hardy. I enjoy growing this American introduction as a cool greenhouse plant. Very free-flowering with enormous orange-red blooms, fading to near white in the centre.

'Hatsugiri'
April   H4

Another of the Kurume Azaleas (see 'Blaauws's Pink'), but this one grows only to 60cm (2ft), while its spread is somewhat wider, at about 90cm (3ft). It is a twiggy little bush, completely reliable in flowering, and looks especially attractive on a rock garden. In April it will present a mass of bright magenta flowers and it is rightly popular for the brilliance of its colour.

'Hino Crimson'
April   H4

(*amoenum* x 'Hinodegiri')

A compact evergreen azalea with small, glossy green leaves among which a mass of bright crimson flowers appears early in the spring. Try to guard it from early spring frost. The foliage turns to attractive shades of bronze or deep red in the autumn, though few of the leaves actually fall.

'Hinodegiri'
April   H4

This azalea was one of 'Wilson's Fifty'. About 1920 the distinguished plant collector E H Wilson selected and took back to America fifty fine hybrids grown by or for Mr Akashi at

'Fascination'

he city of Kurume. But, 'Hinodegiri' had already reached Europe about ten years earlier and had been used by R M Koster during the First World War as a parent of his Malvatica hybrids. The plant earned all this attention with its vivid, purplish-red flowers. The dense, compact bush, is somewhat bigger than 'Hatsugiri', capable of spreading up to 1.5m (5ft) wide. In the autumn, the leaves often take on good colours of red, bronze and orange, but do not fall.

'Hinomayo'
May   H4

Legend says this plant came from the Emperor's garden and was the first Japanese Azalea to be brought to Europe. It was certainly propagated in Holland by van Nes of Boskoop from about 1910. It has exceedingly pretty, delicately-pink flowers entirely covering the bush, which grows at its best in dappled shade.

indicum

The notes on this subject will be found in the 'Tender and Conservatory' section on page 92.

'Iro-Hayama'
May   H4

A small plant, but wide at 105cm (3.5ft). This azalea has light-green leaves and its flowers are white edged with lavender, making it a pleasing and unusual hybrid of the Kurume group.

'Kermesina Rose'
May

If you are looking for something different in evergreen azalea flowers, here is the answer. It has charming small pink flowers, neatly edged in white. Certainly an interesting new hardy plant that will be widely grown.

'Kirin'
May   H3

Being one of the Wilson Kurumes,

'Kirin' is naturally an outstandingly pretty azalea. Its flowers are 'hose-in-hose', deep rose-pink on the outside, and lighter, silvery-pink on the inside. Height is eventually about 1m (3ft) and flowering is in early May. It is not quite hardy, so needs careful placing. This one is often sold as a winter pot-plant, being forced into flowering in January and February.

kiusianum 'K K Khusan'
May   H3

I find the display of pink and white very appealing when this plant produces its mass of flowers late in the spring. It is grown quite extensively on the west coast of America, but I do not believe it is very widely known elsewhere.

'Louise Dowdle'
May/June   H4

A vigorous plant with exceptionally large, tyrian-pink flowers showing a darker blotch. 'Louise Dowdle' is one of the Glen Dale Azaleas, raised in Maryland, USA, it flowers late in May and even into June, thus usefully extending the flowering season of rhododendrons.

'Lullaby'
May/June   H4

Exceptionally large, soft-lilac flowers

with deep-purple markings in the throat. This is a vigorous, upright azalea, flowering quite late in the spring.

'Michael Hill'
June   H4

This pink trailing azalea, flowering well into June, is another interesting subject for growing in tubs or pots. 'Michael Hill' also makes excellent ground cover.

'Mother's Day'
June   H4

Given both the Award of Merit and the Award of Garden Merit, this is one of the best dwarf evergreen azaleas. It was produced in Belgium from a cross between a Kurume hybrid and an Indian Azalea. The flowers of 'Mother's Day' are large, semi-double, dark red and they appear in late May to early June, generally avoiding the late spring frost. The foliage is also an attractive red-bronze colour.

'Niagara'
May/June   H4

A late-flowering white azalea, carrying over from late May into June, so that it avoids damage from late spring frost. The flowers are large with a frilled edge and fairly pronounced green eye.

kiusianum 'K K Khusan'

'Lullaby'

'Orange Beauty'

May   H4

The mass of awards that this hybrid, has received speak for themselves, as does its name, 'Orange Beauty'. It is certainly one of the most popular of the evergreen hybrids. The salmon-orange flowers, which appear in May, are a glorious colour, and are produced on a plant slowly growing to about 1.2m (4ft). The hairy leaves are large for an azalea, and the oldest ones become tinted with red in autumn for some weeks, before they do eventually fall.

'Palestrina'

May   H4

Deservedly winning many awards, this Dutch Vuyk hybrid has starkly white, funnel-shaped flowers with green flashes in the throat. 'Palestrina' blooms in May, and tends to be rather upright in habit, growing to about

1.2m (4ft). Although evergreen, it loses some of its leaves in winter, but they are quickly replaced with new ones in spring.

'Panda'

('Everest' x *kiusianum* white)
May   H4

Surely destined to become one of the most popular white evergreen azaleas, 'Panda' is an excellent introduction from the nursery of Peter and Kenneth Cox at Glendoick in Scotland. It is a compact, free-flowering plant that blooms quite late in the season, avoiding the majority of spring frosts.

quinquefolium

(species)

This evergreen azalea, being different from the others in the section, has been listed as a medium rhododendron as described on page 79.

'Rosebud'

May   H4

This is a Gable hybrid, from Stewartstown, Pennyslvania. It is a very distinctive azalea, with large, double pink flowers, when fully grown it forms a low, rather spreading bush. A very interesting variety for the small garden, but 'Rosebud' can also be forced into early flower and is quite often sold as a winter pot plant.

'Salmon's Leap'

May   H4

An exciting new introduction with soft pink flowers and attractive variegated leaves. This could also be an interesting plant for the conservatory. It will definitely require a sheltered site in the garden.

'Snow'

May   H4

As might be expected, the flowers of

'Louise Dowdle'

his plant are pure white. Their purity seems to be accentuated by a green tinge in the throat, and they are usually double, or hose-in-hose, but sometimes come single. It is worth suggesting, if you have never seen the dazzling effect of a mass of different-coloured evergreen azaleas flowering together, that you may wish to have some whites among them to moderate the effect. If so, make sure to choose one of the right height. This particular Kurume hybrid grows to about 90cm (3ft).

'Squirrel'
('Galathea' x *nakaharae*)
May/June   H4
Good glossy foliage, setting off a mass of small orange-red flowers, makes this an excellent evergreen azalea. What particularly appeals to me about it, as a fairly new introduction from the Cox family's Glendoick nursery,

is the late flowering time, often into June. This avoids any frost problems and also extends the flowering season well into early summer.

'Vuyk's Rosy Red'
May   H4
Low and spreading, attaining a width of about 1.5m (5ft), this old Dutch hybrid has very large flowers 7–8cm (3in) wide or more, red with a deeper

marking in the throat.

'Vuyk's Scarlet'
May   H4
This is another old azalea from the same source. Its large, intensely deep-red flowers take a lot of beating for beauty. With these and its short stature, 80cm (32in) high, it seems indispensable for the small garden or rockery.

'Hino Crimson'

'Kermesina Rose'

'Vuyk's Rosy Red'

'Palestrina'

'Rosebud'

Deciduous azalea species and hybrids for the garden

All the plants listed below can be taken as medium size, except 'Daviesii', which is a little smaller.

'Berryrose'
May   H4

This is a Knap Hill hybrid, from the Exbury nursery, one of the best deciduous kinds, whose rose-pink flowers have a distinctive yellow blotch. The young leaves and shoots are coppery-green in colour.

'Coccinea Speciosa'
May   H4

One of the really old hybrid deciduous azaleas. Introduced before 1846 from Belgium, this was finally given its Award in 1969. As a Ghent hybrid it flowers late, covering itself with a mass of simply brilliant orange-red blooms. These make up in colour and quantity for their smallish size. The height is about 1.5m (5ft), but the spread is more, perhaps 2.1m (7ft).

'Daviesii'
(*viscosum* x *molle*)
May/June   H4–5

Another of the old Ghent hybrids, and still well worth planting. It is more compact than many of the new hybrids, and has unusual, soft grey foliage. Many small trusses of pale-cream flowers appear rather late, towards early summer. The whole plant tends to a spreading, creeping habit that is called stoloniferous. This means it can propagate itself by layering. See page 48.

'Fireball'
May   H4

The fiery orange-red flowers of this azalea make a brilliant complement to its deep red foliage. A really beautiful Knap Hill type from Exbury.

'George Reynolds'
May/June   H4

One of the original Knap Hill deciduous azaleas, and still one of the best. It was introduced by Lionel de

'Berryrose'

'Coccinea Speciosa'

'Hotspur'

others. The colour of the semi-double flowers is deep carmine red, shading out to pale rose pink.

'Hotspur'
May   H4
The deep-orange flowers have a pale yellow flash in the throat. This is one of the original Exbury varieties and continues to be popular.

japonicum
(species)
May   H4
Perhaps it may help the reader if the tangle of nomenclature is straightened out a little at this point. *R japonicum* is an azalea; but it is not a 'Japanese Azalea' – which would be have to be evergreen. It is a member of the *luteum* subseries of deciduous azaleas.

Before reclassification, this plant used to be known as *Azalea mollis*, parent of all the Mollis hybrid azaleas, known for their fine colours. In May it unfolds its abundant funnel-shaped orange-red flowers before the young green leaves appear.

While azaleas are principally renowned for their glorious vivid blooms, some deciduous kinds are also highly decorative in autumn, when their leaves change colour before falling. Our subject is one of these, as can be seen from the picture of *R. luteum* on page 35.

Rothschild who bought a seedling of it from Waterer's in 1922, and used it to breed many new hybrids, notably 'Hotspur'. The very large, deep-yellow flowers have darker orange markings in the throat.

'Gibraltar'
May   H4
One of the best-known of the deciduous azaleas. The buds are an attractive crimson-orange, opening to large flame-orange flowers with slightly frilled petals. Like 'Fireball', it is a post-war Exbury hybrid.

'Harvest Moon'
May   H4
The clear-yellow blooms of this Knap Hill-type hybrid, which originated from Slocock's nursery, have a pronounced deeper-yellow flare in the throat. A well-grown plant looks quite outstanding in May. However, it is not a strong grower, and needs careful positioning and feeding.

'Homebush'
May   H4
The almost-completely round heads of flowers distinguish this old Waterer's Knap Hill azalea from all

'Persil'

'Silver Slipper'

The brilliant-hued flowers which this genus typically presents are designed to be pollinated by day-flying insects which are attracted by colour. Perhaps albino blooms arise as an aberration. In any case, a white azalea in the garden makes a pleasantly cool change from the orange, pink, red and salmon colours, and the distinctive yellow blotch in the throat of 'Oxydol' emphasizes the icy impression.

'Persil'

May   H4

'Persil' is another of the best white deciduous hybrids. Its pure white flowers have a deep yellow blotch in the throat and are large for an azalea, being more than 5cm (2in) wide. Although included in the Knap Hill group, it somewhat resembles the Ghent type where you often see some hose-in-hose flowers amongst the single ones. It was hybridized in the Slocock nursery, whereas 'Oxydol' was from Exbury.

'Klondyke'

May   H4

The golden-yellow flowers of this Exbury-grown Knap Hill hybrid make an outstanding display. This is one of the best hybrids in its group, with large flowers, flushed red on the reverse, also red when in bud, offset by coppery-red leaves and shoots.

luteum

(species)

May   H4

Unlike so many of the rhododendrons and azaleas, this is hardly an exotic plant, so close to Britain does it originate. From Eastern Europe to the Caucasus is its native habitat, but it is now naturalised in parts of the British Isles. Its popularity is deserved for several reasons; the flowers come in delightful shades of yellow, varying from form to form; their stamens extend out of the corolla, rather like those of the honeysuckle, and indeed diffuse a powerful honeysuckle fragrance. The bush reaches its ultimate height of 2m (6ft 6in) quite quickly, keeping an open and delicately twiggy habit. Pruning after flowering will keep it compact. In autumn, the leaves display fiery-red, orange and yellow tints before falling. *R. luteum* is easily grown from seed, and is excellent for naturalizing in woodland.

'Oxydol'

May   H4

White as a colour, if it can be called a colour, is rarely met with in azaleas, or rhododendrons for that matter.

'Homebush'

R. *schlippenbachii*

R. *vaseyi*

schlippenbachii

(species)

April   H4

This azalea species which originates from quite a wide area around North Korea and Manchuria, may grow larger than most deciduous ones, and its wider-open flowers come in an attractive range of pink tints, spotted red in the throat. The blooms appear quite early, even before the leaves, and may be susceptible to late spring frost. The foliage can display interesting colour both in the young growth and in autumn before the leaves fall.

'Silver Slipper'

May   H4

A charming name for a charming plant. Its trumpet-shaped flowers are among the most beautiful adornments of the Knap Hill range, or indeed of azaleas generally. Almost white, with a pink flush and with distinctive yellow markings in the throat, the flowers are accompanied by young leaves and stems all tinted reddish-bronze.

'Strawberry Ice'

May   H4

This excellent and very popular deciduous azalea has deeply-coloured carmine buds which open into warm pink flowers with a yellow flash in the throat. The foliage is attractive in summer, with copper markings.

vaseyi

(species)

May   H4

Covered with a haze of rich-pink flowers late in the spring, this delightful deciduous azalea species from North Carolina has great charm. The individual blooms look like delicate pink butterflies because of their graceful upturned stamens. The leaves give a rich display of colour in the autumn.

viscosum

June   H4

The 'Swamp Honeysuckle' grows wild in eastern north America. It is especially valuable for its late flowering as well as for its delicious fragrance. Sadly, it is seldom available in cultivation. The narrow-tubular flowers, white and sometimes flushed with pink, come out after the leaves. As its common name suggests, it does best in moist soil.

Glossary

Acidity
Sourness, especially of soil; an important factor favourable to rhododendrons and azaleas. Measured in terms of pH.

Alkalinity
Opposite of acidity. A chemical state of the soil, which is adverse to rhododendrons and azaleas. See also Hardness of Water, pH.

Altitude
Height above sea-level. Often a factor segregating different rhododendron species whose places of origin may appear close together on the map.

Apex
Tip or end-point (as of a leaf).

Appressed
Lying flat, or close against (as with leaf-hairs).

Auriculate
Shaped with ear-like lobes (as with leaf shape).

Axillary
Growing from the angle formed between leaf-stalk and stem.

Azalea
Plant belonging to the azalea series of the rhododendron genus.

Azalea Gall
A fungal disease afflicting evergreen azaleas.

Azaleodendron
A hybrid between an azalea and rhododendron of another series.

Bare-root
Plants used to be dug up from nursery beds and sold. It is not done much nowadays (see Container Grown) and the term was never really applicable to rhododendrons. (see Rootball).

Bark-split
A damaging effect of frost on some rhododendrons and azaleas.

Bract
Modified leaf below inflorescence, usually insignificant but in certain instances outshining the flower itself.

Bud
Flower or inflorescence which is formed but not yet open. An attractive winter feature in many rhododendrons and other plants.

Bud blast
A fungal disease afflicting R. ponticum and a few other rhododendrons.

Calcareous
Limy or chalky (of soil or rock), therefore chemically alkaline.

Campanulate
Bell-shaped, referring to flower-form.

Chlorophyll
Characteristic green pigment of plants, enabling them to perform photosynthesis.

Chlorosis
Yellowing of leaves which should be green. A symptom of various maladies.

Ciliate
Fringed with hairs.

Classification
Assignment of a plant into a names class according to the system of Taxonomy.

Clone
Vegetatively propagated progeny of a single individual. All members of a named clone will be genetically identical. See also GREX.

Container grown
Most young plants commercially available now are sold in the container in which they have been growing.

Cordate
Heart-shaped, referring to leaf-shape.

Cotyledon
One of the seed leaves, which are already present in the seed before germination. With rhododendrons, there are two.

Cross
To interbreed genetically different plants. A hybrid so produced.

Cultivar
Member of a cultivated variety which is distinguished by name from other varieties of the same genetic group.

Cutting
Small piece severed from parent especially for the purpose of vegetative propagation.

Defoliation
Loss of leaves, usually resulting from some harmful cause.

Double
(Of flower) with petals multiplied, or supplemented by other flower-parts taking on petal-like form.

Dwarf
For the descriptive list in this book, I have taken an ultimate height of 1 metre as dividing dwarf plants from the medium sized.

Elepidote
Lacing scales. As a noun, this denotes one of the two groups forming the rhododendron genus Elepidotes, which include generally the larger species, which are almost without exception unable to cross-breed with Lepidotes.

Elliptic

In the shape of an ellipse, two dimensionally oval.

Entire

(Of leaf) with a smooth edge, not toothed or cut.

Epigeal

Bearing cotyledons above ground directly upon germination.

Fastigiate

(Of tree or shrub.) Having upward, feather-like pattern of branching.

Fertile

Bearing seeds which are capable of germinating.

Fertilisation

Successful sexual union, whether naturally or artificially achieved. See Insects.

Fibre

Threads of organic matter in the soil, no longer actively decaying.

Forcing

Artificially hastening the maturity (especially flowering) of a plant, usually by a favourable artificial alteration of micro-climate. No harm is implied.

Form

Minor variant of a species. Very often, an unusual and interesting form has been selected and propagated as a named clone.

Frost pocket

Frosty air flows downhill but when trapped, a very cold microclimate is created.

Frost-resistance

Some plants withstand frost better than others. For cold gardens this is a key factor in plant selection.

Fruit

The mature state of the ovary, the seed-bearing organ.

Fungicide

Fungus destroying substance.

Fungus

Moulds and rusts form part of this category of often microscopic plants which grow within chlorophyll by feeding an organic matter. Many types of fungus damage cultivated plants.

Gall

see Azalea Gall.

Gene

Physical particles on the chromosomes which govern inheritance of particular characteristics.

Genus

Group of related species within the system of Taxonomy. Theoretically genera (pl) are supposed to be so defined that differences across generic boundaries are too great for interbreeding to be possible.

Glabrous

Without hair

Glandular

Bearing or relating to cells which have a secreting function.

Glaucous

Apparent colour which is greyish-bluish because of a surface bloom or sheen over a darker true colour.

Grafting

Propagation achieved by physically joining a growing shoot of one plant (scion) into the stem of another (stock).

Grex

All the seedlings resulting from one cross. These are not genetically identical. That is why some hybrids (Carita, Naomi) come in a family of similar names. See Clone.

Ground Cover

Dense use of (usually low) planting, often underneath taller, more open plants, so as to cover up the soil. The purpose may be for visual effect only, but usually is (also) meant to smother and take light from weeds which would otherwise grow there.

Habit of Growth

Inherent mode of growth, characteristic of the type of plant.

Hairs

Filamentary, thread-like surface structures.

Hardiness

Ability to grow in the open all year round. Degrees of this, as indicated by Hardiness Ratings (see page 35) are important in choosing plants.

Note that early flowering plant which are themselves perfectly hardy may lose their blooms whenever caught out by a late frost. Please read the plant descriptions carefully.

Hardness of Water

Alkalinity due to mineral chalk or lime in solution. Most public water supplies in England are somewhat hard and rainwater is preferable for rhododendrons and azaleas. However hard water is much better than no water.

Hirsute

Hairy, especially with long, rough or coarse hairs.

Hose-in-hose

Having a second corolla within the first, giving a double appearance. This is characteristic of many evergreen azaleas.

Humus

Part of the contents of the soil consisting of fully decayed organic matter.

Hybrid

Plant resulting from cross fertilization between genetically different parents, visually of distinct species.

Hybridize

Deliberately to produce hybrids, especially by methodical, programmed hybridizing.

Impressed

Of leaf veins, sunk below surrounding level as though pressed in.

Indumentum

A woolly or hairy covering of the undersides of leaves and sometimes on young shoots. Widely regarded as an attractive characteristic of many rhododendrons for its colour or texture. See also Tomentum.

Inflorescence

The flowers that arise together from a single bud, whether single or multiple. See Truss.

Insects

Rhododendrons generally use insect vectors to transfer pollen for fertilisation. See Nectar..

Lace wing fly (bug)

Insect causing minor discoloured

spotting of leaves in the sun. (Eastern USA).

Lanceolate
Of leaves, spear-shaped.

Lateral
Sideways; on the side.

Lepidote
Scale-bearing. As a noun, this denotes one of the two groups forming the rhododendron genus. Lepidotes, which include generally the smaller species, are almost without exception unable to cross-breed with Elepidotes.

Lobe
A free area of the corolla which is beyond any fused part. See Corolla Tube.

Mildew
See Powdery Mildew

Monotypic
Of a genus, comprising only one representative species.

Morphological
Relating to the form or general structure of the plant.

Mycorrhiza
Root-hairs of a plant functioning in symbiosis with particular soil fungus.

Neutral
Soil-moisture with a ph7 (neutral) is still not acidic enough for rhododendrons.

New Growth
Can be vulnerable to unseasonable frost in some cases. Many rhododendrons offer distinctive new growth as a decorative effect.

Nomenclature
Scientific name of a plant within the system of Taxonomy.

Open Ground
Nurserymen's former method of growing plants in ordinary soil and digging them up for sale during the non-growing season. Now largely obsolete. See Container Grown.

Parentage
Specific identity of the immediate genetic forbears of an individual seedling, taken as being also the parentage of every member of its clone.

Persistent
Of fruits or seed capsules, these remaining attached to the plant after ripening.

pH
(abbr.) Indication of the measurable alkalinity of the soil-moisture in terms of the pressure of Hydrogen ions. Acid soil, suitable for rhododrons has pH below 6.

Photosynthesis
Generation of sugars within the plant by combining carbon dioxide from the air with water. This process, fundamental to almost the whole Plant Kingdom, requires the energy of light and the presence within the plant tissue of chlorophyll (qv).

Phytophthora
A serious fungal disease. Please refer to the relevant chapter.

Pollen
Microspores (comprising four cells in the rhododendron) containing the male gamete which fertilizes the ovule.

Pollination
Transfer of pollen from the anther of its origins to the stigma of the flower to be fertilized. Insects, attracted by nectar, naturally do this for the plant. But if done by human intervention, it is still pollination.

Powdery Mildew
A serious fungal disease. Please refer to the relevant chapter.

Precocious
Flowering before the leaves appear

Prolific
Producing abundantly (esp of offspring).

Propagation
Multiplication of plants, whether sexually or by various other means. See relevant chapter.

Prostrate
Creeping, or growing flat to the ground.

Recessive
Apparently suppressed hereditary characteristic which may reappear in subsequent generations.

Rhachis (rachis)
Axis of the inflorescence.

Root
Underground part of plant which draws moisture and nutrients from the soil.

Rootball
Rhododendrons form a dense shallow mat of roots not extending beyond the spread of the plant. This enables them to be more readily moved than most plants.

Rust
Minor fungal disease causing powdery orange patches under leaves.

Scale
Tiny multicellular disc-like outgrowths from the surfaces of the leaves, shoots and sometimes flower parts in Rhododendrons of the Lepidote group. Their function is to give powerful and versatile control of the rate of transpiration.

Scale-insect
Small insect pest of limpet-like appearance. Please refer to relevant chapter.

Scion
Shoot of one plant cut for grafting into another.

Self sterile
Infertile with its own pollen

Semi-evergreen
Retaining some leaves through winter, but losing some.

Series
Major division of the Rhododendron genus under the prevailing (late 20th century) system of Taxonomy. The azaleas form one of the largest series).

Sessile
With no stalk.

Shade
Different rhododendrons have varied reactions to sunshine and shade. The choice of a plant for a given site should take this factor into consideration.

Shoot
Scientific category defining a group of closely related, inter-breeding individuals or found in the wild,

sharing consistent characteristics, and maintaining distinct differences from other species.

Snow
Heavy snow can endanger rhododendrons as much by its weight as its chilling effect.

Species
Scientific category defining a group of closely related, interbreeding individuals or found in the wild, sharing consistent characteristics, and maintaining distinct differences from other species.

Sport
Individual specimen, whether series or hybrid, which deviates in a marked and unexpected way from its genetic type. Where it presents desirable changes, a sport can be propagated (eg 'Bruce Brechtbill').

Sterile
Unable to reproduce sexually. Many hybrids are sterile but can be propagated vegetatively.

Stock
A plant, the root and stem of which are to be used to sustain one or more shoots grafted on to it.

Stoloniferous
Growing by suckers or by striking root from basal branches where they touch the soil.

Sub-section
Subdivision within a Section. This refers to revised systems of classification by Brickell, Cullen and Chamberlain in the late 1970's. It remains to be seen how all this work is assimilated with the revision by Sleumer (1949) and by the Philipsons (1975) and still in progress.

Sub-series
Subdivision within a Series. This was only used within the larger more complex series under the "Balfourain" classification of 1930, which is in process of being superseded. See Sub-section.

Sun-tolerance
Rhododendrons and azaleas do vary in this respect for various reasons. This is mentioned for special cases in the descriptive lists.

Symbiosis
Close, mutually beneficial relationship between the life-processes of two different plants. See Mycorrhiza.

Taxonomy
System for co-ordinating the classification required on scientific grounds with the appropriate nomenclature for the plants.

Terminal Bud
This is a very important growth point, because it is normally around the terminal bud of a branch that the most active new growth will arise after flowering.

Tissue culture
Scientifically known as Meristematic propagation, this is a very new, high-tech system of vegetative propagation, discussed in the relevant chapter.

Tomentum
Woolly or hairy covering on upper side of leaf. See also Indumentum.

Transpiration
Emission of water vapour through the pores of the leaves. This vital process is so important to rhododendrons that they have special organs to control it in many species and the root system also is adapted to take in the large amount of water lost by transpiration.

Truss
Cluster of flowers arising as one inflorescence from a single flower bud, taking a different characteristic form in each rhododendron.

Ultimate Height
A very important consideration in selecting a rhododendron for a particular garden site.

Variegation
Diversified leaf colouration. Not many rhododendrons have this feature, but those that have offer great garden interest.

Variety
Plant recognizably differing from the species or hybrid to which it belongs sufficiently to acquire its own varietal name.

Vegetative
Growth or reproduction not involving any sexual process.

Viscid
Sticky, as with the secretion of the stigma.

Weevils
Harmful insect pest. Please see relevant chapter.

Wind
Some rhododendrons are well adapted to withstand windy conditions, but many require a degree of shelter.

Zygomorphic
Hairy bilateral symmetry.

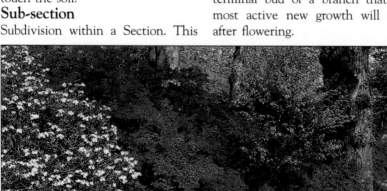

R. *luteum* and 'Hatsugiri'

Nurseries specialising in the sale of rhododendrons and azaleas

Bridgemere Garden World
Bridgemere
Nantwich
Cheshire
CW5 7QB

Exbury Enterprises Limited
Exbury
Nr Southampton
Hants

Glendoick Gardens Limited
Perth
Scotland
PH2 7NS

Hydon Nurseries
Clock Barn Lane
Hydon Heath
Godalming
Surrey

Millais Nurseries
Crosswater Farm
Churt
Farnham
Surrey
GU10 2JN

G Reuthe Limited
Crown Point Nursery
Sevenoaks Road
Ightham
Nr Sevenoaks
Kent

Starborough Nursery
Starborough Road
Marsh Green
Edenbridge
Kent
TN8 5RB

Gardens to visit for rhododendrons and azaleas

Bodnant Gardens
Tal-y-cafyn
Gwynedd

Brodick Castle
Isle of Arran
Bute

Exbury Gardens
Exbury
Southampton

Isabella Plantation
Richmond Park
Richmond
Surrey

Powis Castle
Welshpool
Powys

Royal Botanic Garden
Inverleith Row
Edinburgh

Royal Botanic Garden
Kew
Surrey

Royal Horticultural Society
Wisley
Nr Woking
Surrey

Savill Gardens
Windsor Great Park
Berkshire

Trewithen Gardens
Nr Truro
Cornwall

Wakehurst Place
Ardingly
Sussex

Mixed azaleas

'Wally Miller'

'Squirrel'

'Dopey'

'Salmon's Leap'

'Trewithen Orange'

'Iro-Hayama'

Index